On the Side of the Poor

ON THE SIDE OF THE POOR
The Theology of Liberation

GUSTAVO GUTIÉRREZ
and
CARDINAL GERHARD LUDWIG MÜLLER

Translated by
Robert A. Krieg and James B. Nickoloff

ORBIS BOOKS
Maryknoll, New York

ORBIS BOOKS
Maryknoll, New York 10545

Fathers and Brothers
MARYKNOLL™

Founded in 1970, Orbis Books endeavors to publish works that enlighten the mind, nourish the spirit, and challenge the conscience. The publishing arm of the Maryknoll Fathers and Brothers, Orbis seeks to explore the global dimensions of the Christian faith and mission, to invite dialogue with diverse cultures and religious traditions, and to serve the cause of reconciliation and peace. The books published reflect the views of their authors and do not represent the official position of the Maryknoll Society. To learn more about Maryknoll and Orbis Books, please visit our website at www.maryknollsociety.org.

Translation copyright © 2015 by Orbis Books

Published by Orbis Books, Maryknoll, New York 10545-0302.

Originally published as *An der Seite der Armen: Theologie der Befreiung.* © 2004 by Sankt Ulrich Verlag GmbH, Augsburg.

Chapters by Gerhard Ludwig Müller and foreword by Josef Sayer were translated from German by Robert A. Krieg; chapters by Gustavo Gutiérrez were translated from Spanish by James B. Nickoloff.

Grateful acknowledgment is made to Oxford University Press for permission to reprint the translation of Gustavo Gutiérrez's "The Situation and Tasks of Liberation Theology Today," which originally appeared in Joerg Rieger, ed., *Opting for the Margins: Postmodernity and Liberation in Christian Theology,* © 2003 by the American Academy of Religion.

Manufactured in the United States of America.

Library of Congress Cataloging-in-Publication Data

Gutierrez, Gustavo, 1928-
  [An der Seite der Armen. English]
  On the side of the poor : the theology of liberation / Gustavo Gutierrez and Cardinal Gerhard Ludwig Muller ; translated by Robert A. Krieg and James B. Nickoloff.
    pages cm
    Includes bibliographical references and index.
    ISBN 978-1-62698-115-7 (pbk.)
    1. Liberation theology. 2. Civil rights—Religious aspects—Christianity.
  I. Muller, Gerhard Ludwig. II. Title.
  BT83.57.G85313 2015
  230'.0464—dc23
                                        2014035646

Contents

Foreword   vii
Josef Sayer

1. THEOLOGY: AN ECCLESIAL FUNCTION   1
   Gustavo Gutiérrez
   Evangelization and Theology   2
   A Moment for Latin America   4
   To Proclaim the Reign Today   7

2. LIBERATING EXPERIENCE: A STIMULUS
   FOR EUROPEAN THEOLOGY   11
   Gerhard Ludwig Müller
   A New Understanding of Theology:
       Theological Reflection in the Service
       of God's Liberating Praxis   13
   Liberation Theology in the Energy Field
       between Latin America and Europe   22
   A New Sense of "We" in the Church and
       in the Service of the Salvation of Others   28

3. THE SITUATION AND TASKS
   OF LIBERATION THEOLOGY TODAY   32
   Gustavo Gutiérrez
   Three Great Contemporary Challenges to Faith   33
   The Modern (and Postmodern) World   34
   Religious Pluralism   37
   An Inhuman and Anti-evangelical Poverty   38
   Current Tasks   43

The Complexity of the World of the Poor   43
Globalization and Poverty   47
Deepening Spirituality   50

4. LIBERATION THEOLOGY IN CONTEXT   54
   Gerhard Ludwig Müller
   The Necessity for a Theology of Liberation   54
   The Original Theological Approach
       of Liberation Theology   57
   Liberation Theology in Its Realization   65
   A Critique of Liberation Theology:
       Its Merits and Limits   76

5. WHERE WILL THE POOR SLEEP?   83
   Gustavo Gutiérrez
   Theology and the Proclamation of the Gospel   84
   Toward a Planetary Economy   93
   Proclaiming the Reign   114
   Conclusion   132

6. THE COMMON FUTURE OF THE CHURCH   134
   Gerhard Ludwig Müller

Index   139

Foreword

Josef Sayer

Two theologians have written this book: the well-known Peruvian liberation theologian Gustavo Gutiérrez and Gerhard Ludwig Müller, the former professor of theology from Munich who in 2002 was named the bishop of Regensburg.[1] These are two theologians out of two different worlds of experience. Nevertheless, there are important parallels and common fundamental convictions in the thinking of these two persons who are friends with each other. In this regard, it's noteworthy that Gustavo Gutiérrez concelebrated at the Mass when Gerhard Ludwig Müller was consecrated a bishop.[2]

Translator's note: Josef Sayer (b. 1941) is a German Catholic priest and theologian who engaged in pastoral ministry in Cuzco, Peru, beginning in 1981. From 1997 to 2012, he served as the president of *Misereor*, the German Catholic bishops' international organization for human development in Africa, Asia, Latin America, and Oceana.

1. Translator's note: Gerhard Ludwig Müller (b. 1947) became a professor of theology at the University of Munich in 1986. After ten years as the bishop of Regensburg, he was appointed by Pope Benedict XVI as the prefect of the Congregation for the Doctrine of the Faith on July 2, 2012. He was named a cardinal by Benedict XVI on February 22, 2013.

2. Translator's note: Gustavo Gutiérrez (b. 1928) is a priest and theologian. Ordained to the priesthood in the Archdiocese of Lima, Peru, in 1959, he joined the Dominican Order in 1999. On September 12, 2013, he was warmly greeted by Pope Francis in Rome. Shortly before this meeting, which Cardinal Müller attended, the present book of essays by Gutiérrez and Müller, *An der Seite der Armen*, was published in Italian.

I met Gustavo Gutiérrez for the first time in 1978 on the occasion of an interview. I came away with a twofold impression: here is a person who is passionately struggling with the question, How can someone speak about the love of God in light of both the misery of the poor and also injustice in the world? This basic question of the theology of liberation has remained with me ever since.

And the second impression from that meeting was this: an interview is an unsuitable method for meeting Gustavo Gutiérrez. During my subsequent work in Peru, I have had many opportunities to come to know Gutiérrez in lectures and courses as well as at Masses and among the poor. Nearness to those who live in poverty characterizes him. Along with his theological activity—or, one must more appropriately say, *because* of it—he is a priest in a slum community. In his theological reflections he always surprises people with examples out of his praxis. Here is a case in point: "A woman in a slum has taught me that the opposite of joy is not suffering but sadness. Whoever succumbs to sadness sees no future, lacks hope. The suffering people, the poor have hope and their liturgical celebrations are filled with beauty, hope, and joy. The poor celebrate in joyful festivities."

Characteristic of Gutiérrez is also something that he learned from the poor: he sees them truly as personal subjects. Ever since he returned to Peru from his studies in Europe, their lives have not allowed him to find peace. His special ability for observation and analysis of social realities and also of the living conditions of the poor led him to become the "father of liberation theology." In 1968 he was asked to give a lecture, corresponding to the spirit of that time, entitled the "theology of development." He shaped this theme in light of his vision into his lecture on the "theology of liberation." Afterward, he enlarged the basic idea of this presentation into the book of the same name, and in the course of the years he has created a scholarly oeuvre that has left its mark on the history of theology.[3]

---

3. Editor's note: Gustavo Gutiérrez's *Teología de la liberación: Perspectivas* was originally published in 1971. The English translation, *A Theology of Liberation,* was published in 1973 (Maryknoll, NY: Orbis Books, 1973; 2nd ed.

For many people, this work by Gutiérrez represents one of the most innovative theological initiatives of the twentieth century. As every "new" theology must do, the theology of liberation must give an account of itself and its view of the church with regard to how the essential elements of the Christian tradition are known and effective within it. The theology of liberation has extended this demonstration without ceasing through the works of Gutiérrez, in which the attentiveness to the poor is united with a deep—in the best sense—Catholic spirituality and mysticism. The epochal significance of the theology of liberation is situated in that it has helped the church once again to discover, as its substantial imperative, its dedication to justice and the holistic proclamation of the Good News for and especially by the poor.

The central insights of the theology of liberation—which involves reflection on the growing chasm between the poor and the rich and also between the structures of sin and God's preferential option for the poor—are fruitful above all in the teaching and preaching of Pope John Paul II. When someone reproachfully declares to Gustavo Gutiérrez that the theology of liberation will hardly be discussed in the future since its best years are now behind it, the Peruvian theologian smiles and answers that there is one individual who surely continued to speak about it: Pope John Paul II himself insisted without interruption upon the preferential option for the poor and their rights. This insistence came to the pope apart from the name "theology of liberation." Time and again, Gutiérrez stresses this association. For him it concerns the actual reality

---

1988). Among his other books in English are *The Power of the Poor in History* (Maryknoll, NY: Orbis Books, 1983); *We Drink from Our Own Wells: The Spiritual Journey of a People* (Maryknoll, NY: Orbis Books, 1983); *On Job: God-Talk and the Suffering of the Innocent* (Maryknoll, NY: Orbis Books, 1987); *The Truth Shall Make You Free: Confrontations* (Maryknoll, NY: Orbis Books, 1990); *The God of Life* (Maryknoll, NY: Orbis Books, 1991); *Las Casas: In Search of the Poor of Jesus Christ* (Maryknoll, NY: Orbis Books, 1993); *Sharing the Word through the Liturgical Year* (Maryknoll, NY: Orbis Books, 1997); *The Density of the Present: Selected Writings* (Maryknoll, NY: Orbis Books, 1999).

of people in poverty. So long as their state of affairs is wretched and truly miserable, it is necessary to pursue the intention of the theology of liberation.

In this perspective, the theology of liberation, which some people often declare to be dead, stands at the beginning of a long path forward. In the decades since its beginning in 1968, it has shown itself to be impressively successful—above all, in the Catholic Church of Latin America but not only there. In 1968 the bishops of Latin America came together in the city of Medellín, Columbia. This conference is regarded as the official birth of a movement that draws out of the gospel not only the imperative to help the poor but also to transform the directions of society in concrete ways.

The widespread poverty and injustice in this "Catholic" continent—as also elsewhere in the world—are not overcome in great measure. However, the attitude toward this poverty and misery has been decisively transformed from within by theology and the church. The church and theology have themselves become conscious that the growing chasm between the poor and the rich represents not only a consequence of more or less accidental economic and social conditions but also an expression of structural sin, which goes contrary to the order of creation and is ultimately an affront to God—indeed, ultimately a blasphemy. For the theology of liberation, the existence of poverty and injustice is not only a social-ethical issue beside other issues. Rather, the theology of liberation makes clear that the question of God comes into play here. The existence of poverty and injustice concerns not only the Seventh Commandment but also and first of all the First Commandment (Exodus 20:15; 20:2-6). The absolute claim of the marketplace's gods, to which the basic day-to-day concerns of a great portion of the human family is subjugated, stands in contradiction to the acknowledgment of the one Lord of the world and history who has shown and demonstrated that the true God takes up the side of the poor and excluded.

Gustavo Gutiérrez has founded a theology that takes its point of departure from the experience of the poor with God and from

"God's experience" with the poor. It asks, how can we speak about the love of God in light of the misery of the poor? How can hope exist among the poor? In the theological writings of Gustavo Gutiérrez there occurs critical reflection on—and also *by*—the poor of Peru and the world about their past, their present, and their future. Without doubt, this critical reflection about the widespread injustice and misery of the poor could be depressing. Indeed, it could lead to despair if the poor were not in fact viewing their past, their present, and above all even their future in the light of their faith in God—and further if they had not already experienced God as the one God who is on their side. In the theology of liberation, Gustavo Gutiérrez has communicated this hope of the poor and has brought it into a theological language. He has made it understandable to us that the poor have a future—not somehow because they are "morally" good or because they possess wonderful qualities and abilities, but because God is good and God wants it to be so. In Jesus Christ, God has demonstrated God's preferential option for the poor.

Gerhard Ludwig Müller came to know Gustavo Gutiérrez in 1988 in the context of a five-week theological seminar in Peru for German-speaking theology professors. After an intensive group preparation and study of the theological work of Gustavo Gutiérrez, these professors went to Peru and plunged into the social and pastoral realities of the slum parishes as well as into the rural communities of peasant farmers in Peru's high Andes. After a further intensive phase of theological reflection on this experience of praxis, there occurred a week-long intensive workshop with Gustavo Gutiérrez in Lima. These jam-packed days of theological discussion with Gutiérrez formed not only the foundation of a continuing relationship and friendship between the two theologians, but they also inaugurated Müller's orientation toward the church and theology in Latin America.

What is highly unusual for a professor at a German university became for Müller a recurring taken-for-granted activity. Over a period of fifteen years, he spent six to eight weeks in Latin America every year during his breaks between semesters. Here he taught in various seminaries, above all in Cuzco, Peru; he held summer courses for seminarians, and—what is especially noteworthy—he entered into the everyday realities of the poor. Bishop Müller lived for week-long periods in the peasant farmers' parishes, located at heights of 10,000 to 14,000 feet. During these times, he shared in the hard and deprived lives of these poor people. He visited the unfrequented villages at the end of steep mountain paths. And, he slept on the packed-down earth in the mud-brick huts of the peasant farmers. Latin American theology in the sense of the theology of liberation demands learning firsthand the existential reality of people in poverty and grasping this reality as the reference point of theological reflection. To engage in this kind of theology demands faith and closely connects someone to life.

Müller concretely and fully brought into this activity what he discussed in many meetings with Gutiérrez. His origins in a working-class family in Germany that had to endure deprivation after the Second World War helped Müller to share in the existential reality of the poor. In his many lectures in Europe and in a series of writings, Müller has appealed for a better understanding of the church and theology of Latin America, especially on behalf of theology as Gustavo Gutiérrez has developed it.

If the theology of liberation, as Gutiérrez teaches it, is closely related to the specific relationships and realities in Latin America, it nevertheless simultaneously makes clear—as Müller seeks to show in his writings on this theme—that the church in general cannot withdraw from the world into itself; it cannot be interested only in its own members. The church has an obligation to the entire human family and the concrete society in which the church lives and exists. To be Christian means also to stand up for the political, economic, social, and cultural rights of people and for their dignity as God's children—and thus for a humane society.

The book before us, *On the Side of the Poor: The Theology of Liberation*, is the fruit of considerations by both theologians, Gutiérrez and Müller. It sheds light on the role of the church in the present age with its globalization of the "neoliberal" [completely free-market] approach that is one-sidedly fixed on economics [see Müller's essay "Liberating Experience," note 9]. With the collapse of the Iron Curtain and the demise of communist dictators, many people prophesied the definitive rise of capitalism. Nevertheless, this far-reaching, one-sided economic globalization must be illumined and evaluated in the light of social justice, as Pope John Paul II did not tire of stressing in his social teachings and in his many speeches during his travels.

In this regard, one must respect the preferential option for the poor and the view of reality in the light of the Bible. It is here that a Christian theology of liberation grounds its starting point for today. Gutiérrez elucidates this reality, especially [below] in his comprehensive essay entitled "Where Will the Poor Sleep?," which he fashioned in the context of a theological, three-day colloquium in a small circle with Cardinal Ratzinger, then the prefect of the Congregation for the Doctrine of the Faith. Subsequently, in his book *The Salt of the Earth* (1996 in German) Cardinal Ratzinger explicitly refers to Gustavo Gutiérrez when he writes: "We have entered into a dialogue with him—part of which I personally led—and, as a result, have come to a better understanding."

This dialogue helped us to understand Gutiérrez, and he came to see the one-sided character of his [early] work. As a result, he has developed his thought into a form of "liberation theology" with the right content and with a form capable of wider integration into theology.

The book at hand asks about the significance of the theology of liberation for contemporary theology in general and for church life today, and it accepts that the theology of liberation is a necessary and integral ecclesial undertaking. In his "Message to the World," shortly before the start of the Second Vatican Council, Pope John XXIII spoke about the church as "preeminently the church of the poor." The first fruits of these observations were the council's Dogmatic Constitution on the Church, *Lumen gentium*, and its Pastoral Constitution on the Church in the Modern World, *Gaudium et spes*. Afterward, this fundamental—and social—stimulus of

Vatican II brought about the theology of liberation in the church of Latin America. As long as there remain groundless injustices, and illnesses that lead to the deaths of the poor who do not receive medical treatment because of injustice, and as long as there are other structural prejudices in the form of more than 830 million hungry people around the world, and until God's kingdom is fully present in the world, there also must and will be the theology of liberation, for God in Jesus is liberating all people to freedom (see Galatians 5:1).

—*Translated by Robert A. Krieg*

Chapter 1

Theology: An Ecclesial Function

Gustavo Gutiérrez

I would like to present here some thoughts about how I see the present role and future tasks of theological reflection in the life of the church present in Latin America and the Caribbean. My intention is to elucidate what I have stated on other occasions and thus to clarify certain concepts in a sphere where it is easy to fall into oversimplifications and even erroneous ways of understanding theological work. The role of theology is not in fact to forge an ideology that would justify social and political positions already taken but rather to help believers to let themselves be judged by the Word of the Lord. Theology cannot therefore give up the critical function of faith vis-à-vis every historical realization. I begin from the conviction that the theological task is a vocation that arises and is exercised in the heart of the ecclesial community. Indeed, its starting point is the gift of faith in which we welcome the truth of the Word of God, and its contributions are at the service of the evangelizing mission of the church.

This ecclesial location gives theology its raison d'être, determines its scope, nurtures it with the sources of revelation—Scripture and Tradition—enriches it with the recognition of the charisma of the

---

Originally published in *Páginas* 130 (1994) 10-17; English translation published in James Nickoloff, ed., *Gustavo Gutiérrez: Essential Writings* (Maryknoll, NY: Orbis Books, 1996).

magisterium and dialogue with the magisterium, and puts it in contact with other ecclesial functions.

Evangelization and Theology

What is the role of theology in the evangelizing responsibility that is incumbent upon the whole church? "Theology," says the "Instruction on the Ecclesial Vocation of the Theologian" of the Congregation for the Doctrine of the Faith, "offers its contribution so that the faith might be communicated. Appealing to the understanding of those who do not yet know Christ, it helps them to seek and find faith" (7). The missionary perspective, anxious about the aspirations and concerns of those who are far from, or do not share, the Christian faith, gives the deepest meaning to the effort to understand faith.

Within this dynamism—the dynamism of a "truth which tends toward being communicated"—lies the theological task. Theology is a task carried out in the church convoked by the Word. From there, from "within the church" (as the Instruction puts it), the truth that frees (see John 8:32) is proclaimed—salvation in Jesus Christ—and theological reflection is carried out. This is what the Latin American bishops called "the prophetic ministry of the church" when they gathered in Santo Domingo in 1992: to this ministry belongs the service that theologians must offer (33). Its content is the proclamation of Christ and of his integral liberation, the proclamation that must be made in a language faithful to the message and that can speak to our contemporaries. This is the very point of the theological contribution: this is why it must enter into dialogue with the mentality of the culture of those who listen to the Word. In this way it will be able to contribute efficaciously to a pastoral practice that motivates those to whom it is directed to follow the witness and teachings of Jesus.

In this task "the theologian, without ever forgetting that he or she is a member of the People of God, must respect it and commit himself or herself to give them a teaching which does not injure in any way the doctrine of the faith." Otherwise theologians run the risk that the pressing needs of the moment may make it hard to see the requirements of the message in its entirety. They will not fulfill their function of service to the evangelizing of the church and its pastors. Indeed, "the freedom proper to theological reflection is exercised within the faith of the church."

Theology is a speaking about God in the light of faith, a language about one who is, in truth, its only theme. We ought to approach the mystery of God with respect and humility; but in a biblical perspective, mystery does not signify something that should remain secret. Rather, mystery should be spoken and communicated. To be revealed belongs to the very essence of mystery (see Romans 16:25-26). Theology, then, becomes a "science of Christian revelation."

At the same time theologians must be aware that their efforts cannot exhaust the significance of the word contained in Scripture and transmitted by the living tradition of the church in which the charisma of the magisterium is located. Furthermore, "the deposit of faith" present in the church is not limited to answering our queries; it also raises new questions and constantly requires of us an examination of our faith. On the other hand, speaking about God takes place in a constantly changing historical reality in which the ecclesial community lives. No dimension of human existence—which itself is lived in the midst of complex social situations—escapes the condition of being a disciple of Jesus. From this reality arise constant challenges to the discourse on faith. For this reason, the episcopal conference at Santo Domingo, locating itself in its own Latin American environment, speaks of a theological labor that would promote "work in favor of social justice, human rights, and solidarity with the poorest" (33). These are urgent necessities among us.

For these reasons theological language contains much that is approximate: it must therefore always be open to renovation from new perspectives, further precision of concepts, and the correction of formulations. Similarly, there is the permanent emergence of new paths in our speech about God that seeks to express revealed truth in appropriate terms. All this is required along with the clear conviction that—according to a traditional affirmation—no theology can be identified with the faith. Theological pluralism within the unity of faith is an old fact in the church. In this context different theologies are useful and important efforts but on the condition that they do not consider themselves unique or indispensable and that they be aware of their role of modestly serving the primary tasks of the church.

A Moment for Latin America

When Christian faith, received and lived out in the church, experiences new challenges to its communication to others, theology asks itself (as it is always called to do) about the relevance of its reflection on the revealed message. There are numerous historical witnesses to this fact. It is the moment to renew this reflection, going once again to the inexhaustible sources of faith that feed the life of the church.

Poverty is a theme of the Gospels and a challenge that has always been present throughout the church's history. But the denunciations of Medellín ("inhuman misery"), Puebla ("poverty opposed to the gospel"), and Santo Domingo ("intolerable extremes of misery") made the situation of poverty, which the great majority of the population of Latin America and the Caribbean suffers, appear in all its harshness before our eyes. It was a matter of an age-old reality but one that pounded the human and Christian conscience in a new way and that for the same reason raised demanding questions for the ecclesial task. The "others" of a society that marginalizes and excludes them became present, demanding solidarity. The root question—how to say to the poor, to the least of society, that God loves them?—has demonstrated its fruitfulness in the pastoral action of the church and in the theological path undertaken to respond to it.

In the face of unjust and premature death which poverty implies, "the noble combat for justice" (Pius XII) acquires dramatic and urgent characteristics. To be aware of this is a question of clarity and honesty. It is necessary, moreover, to overcome the mentality that places these facts in an exclusively political field in which faith has little or nothing to say; this attitude expresses the "divorce between faith and life," which Santo Domingo sees still today as capable of "producing clamorous situations of injustice, social inequality, and violence" (24). However, to recognize social conflicts as a fact must not in any way signify that social conflict is being promoted as a method of change in society. Thus we cannot accept "the programmed class struggle" (John Paul II, *Laborem exercens*, 11).

We are without a doubt on controversial and slippery terrain. The risk of reductionism (or of expressions that can be interpreted as reductionistic) is thus limiting and threatening. It is easy to be absorbed by the emotional aspects of the situation, to experience a certain fascination with something new, or to overestimate the value of the social sciences. The social sciences are necessary if we are to understand socioeconomic reality, but they represent efforts still in the beginning stages. In view of this, to speak of a scientific understanding of the social universe cannot be considered something definite or apodictic, nor as something completely free of ideological connections.

As for the distinction among three levels in the notion of liberation, Puebla therefore alerts us that "the unity of these three planes" implies that "the mystery of the death and resurrection of Jesus Christ must be lived out on the three planes . . . without making any one of them exclusive" (326). This is the integral liberation in Christ that leads us to full communion with God and others (see LG 1). Social and political liberation should not in any way hide the final and radical significance of liberation from sin which can only be a work of forgiveness and of God's grace. It is important then to refine our means of expression in order to avoid confusion in this matter.

We must pay attention to these dangers and reaffirm the proper and direct level of the gospel; its content is the reign, but the reign must be accepted by people who live in history and consequently the proclamation of a reign of love, peace, and justice impinges on life together in society. Nevertheless, the demands of the gospel go beyond the political project of building a different society. Society will be just, and in a certain sense new, to the degree that it places the dignity of the human person at its center—a dignity that for a Christian has its ultimate foundation in the condition of being the "image of God," which Christ saves by reestablishing the friendship between human beings and God.

Conflictive social realities cannot make us forget the requirements of a universal love that does not recognize boundaries of social class, race, or gender. The affirmation that the human person is the agent of his or her own destiny in history must be made in such a way that the gratuitous initiative of God in the salvific process—the ultimate meaning of the historical evolution of humanity—may be clearly seen. Indeed, the gift of God "who loved us first" (1 John 4:19) frames and gives rise to human action as a free response to that love.

It is possible to go astray in these matters, and in fact this has happened. Nor have misunderstandings been lacking in the face of new themes and new languages. In this way a debate over the theology of liberation arose which even flowed beyond the world of the church and into the wide and stormy world of the media. Nevertheless, beyond appearances and arduous discussions, a profound process was taking place in those years, characterized by a serious and respectful confrontation, well-founded objections, requests for necessary refinements from those who have authority in the church to do so, recognition of the value of being sensitive to the sign of the times which the aspiration to liberation signifies, a legitimate presentation of doubts, and interest in a theology close to the base Christian communities.

All this leads us to see that the effort to capture new realities theologically has to be constantly clarified. Imperfections of language must be overcome, and inexact formulations must be corrected by concepts that do not give rise to errors in matters concerning the doctrine of the faith. Indeed, theological reflection always carries the imprint of the moment and of the circumstances in which it is formulated. This is true in particular for the effort undertaken in Latin America in these years when it was necessary to confront difficult situations, respond to unheard-of challenges to the understanding of the faith, and be able to reach—with the missionary spirit proper to theology—those who do not perceive the significance of the gospel for these realities and for their lives.

It is important above all to be clear about these risks and limitations, to listen with humility to divergent opinions. This attitude follows—it is appropriate to note it—from understanding the meaning of theological work as a service to the evangelizing mission of the entire church to which I have already referred. In theology it is necessary to be ever ready, in the words of John Paul II, to "modify one's own opinions" in function of one's service to "the community of believers." This is the meaning of theological works; this is why it may rightly be affirmed, as the "Letter on the Formation of Future Priests" puts it, that theology "cannot rescind from the doctrine and lived experience in the sphere of the church in which the magisterium authentically watches over and interprets the deposit of faith."

To Proclaim the Reign Today

For all these reasons, and because the process has been complex and difficult but simultaneously rich, a fundamental perspective has opened up a path that carries with it the best of the ecclesial experience of this period. I refer to the preferential option for the poor, which, born of the experience and practice of the Latin American Christian communities, was first expressed at Medellín and then explicitly embraced at Puebla. As we know, this focus is today part of the universal magisterium of the church, as numerous texts of John Paul II and of diverse non-Latin American episcopacies attest. If something should remain from this period of Latin American and church history, it is precisely this option as a demanding commitment, an expression of a love that is always new, and the axis of a new evangelization of the continent.

A series of economic, political, and ecclesial events, as much worldwide as Latin American or national, makes people think that the stage in which the theological reflection recalled a few pages ago came to be born is now coming to an end. The years that have passed were, on the one hand, stimulating and creative, but tense and conflictive on the other. In the face of new situations (the worsening of poverty and the end of certain political projects, for example), many earlier discussions do not respond to current challenges.

Everything would seem to indicate that a different period is beginning. The collaboration of all in facing the enormous questions that the reality of Latin America presents us becomes more and more necessary. There is a reconstitution of the social fabric within which we had sought to place the proclamation of the reign of God, a reconstitution that requires new liberating practices. These must be careful not to fall into the "verticalism of a disembodied spiritual union with God or into a simple existential personalism ... nor, even less, into socioeconomic-political horizontalism" (Puebla, 329). Both deviations, each in its own way, distort at the same time the transcendence and the immanence of the reign of God.

The summoning tone of the Santo Domingo texts responds to this requirement and thus makes an energetic call to all to participate in the new evangelization of the continent. This concern was present since the preparations for Medellín, but it took on new strength with the vigorous call of John Paul II in Haiti (1983), the poorest and most forgotten country of Latin America. Directing himself to CELAM, the pope spoke of "a new evangelization—new in its zeal, in its methods, in its expression." Santo Domingo made this perspective one of its central themes and one of its primary pastoral directions. The theological reflection formulated in the Latin American context finds here fertile ground in its collaboration with the evangelizing task of the church. Making use of successes and avoiding failures of previous years, our discourse on the faith should help us to find the route and the language to proclaim to "the poor of this continent" the need for the "gospel of radical and integral liberation"; not to do so, adds John Paul II, would be to cheat and disillusion the poor.

Santo Domingo takes up a second theme from which it deduces an important pastoral direction: *human promotion*. This is not something foreign or extrinsic to evangelization. In recent years numerous texts of the magisterium have vigorously reminded us that to promote human dignity is part of the evangelizing task. It is dignity called into question by "the most devastating and humiliating scourge that Latin America and the Caribbean are experiencing" and constituted by "the growing impoverishment" of millions of Latin Americans—the consequence in large part of the "policies of the neoliberal type" which predominate on the continent (Santo Domingo, 179).

The depth of the problem is such that it calls the entire church with no exceptions to face it. Biblical reflection on poverty and the experiences of solidarity of previous years are of great usefulness here, but this must not hide what is distinct or delicate in the present situation. The renovation of the church's social teaching energetically undertaken by John Paul II not only offers guidelines for an authentic and contemporary social harmony and for the construction of a just and new society with total respect for human life and dignity, but will also enrich the theological task and provide a fertile field of study pertinent to the social and historical context of Latin America. These texts remind us that the values of peace, justice, and liberty are not only goals of a social commitment but that they ought to inspire, beginning now, the methods we employ for achieving a human society that respects the rights of all.

The new evangelization will have to be an *inculturated evangelization*. "Inculturation" is a new term for designating an old reality, which, for the Christian, carries resonances of incarnation. The Word must incarnate itself in diverse worlds, situations, and cultures. Despite this, its transcendence is not affected; rather, it is reaffirmed. This perspective has put a finger right on the wound in a continent of such great racial and cultural diversity. The cultures and values of the different indigenous peoples and of the black population of Latin America constitute a great treasure that must be appreciated and respected by those who have the responsibility for proclaiming the gospel. We are face to face with an immense and urgent task that has scarcely been initiated and with a stimulating challenge to theological reflection.

These are, then, three themes, three primary pastoral directions (see Santo Domingo, 287-301), and thus three spheres of theological reflection that, as I have pointed out, seek to be at the service of the proclamation of the "gospel of liberation."

To take up these perspectives is to renew "the evangelical and preferential option for the poor, following the example and the words of the Lord Jesus" (Santo Domingo, 180). Christ is, indeed, the ultimate foundation of this option and of the pastoral directions mentioned. As the "living Son of God," he is "the unique reason for our life and the source of our mission" (Santo Domingo, 296).

For this reason the preferential option for the poor not only demands that we seek to know, seriously and responsibly, the reality and the causes of poverty: not only does such an option lead us to make our pastoral action more effective and to deepen our theological reflection. It also ought to mark our spirituality—that is, our following of Jesus Christ, who is "the way, the truth, and the life" (John 14:6). His life, his death, and his resurrection put their imprint on the course in history taken by the church and by every Christian.

Like every believer, the theologian must undertake the discipleship of Jesus. For this purpose, she (or he) will, like Mary, have to preserve "all these things in her heart" (Luke 2:51), that is, the deeds and words in which God is revealed. Whatever the historical context may be in which we live, no matter how tense the situations that must be faced, this discipleship signifies leading a life nourished—as John frequently says—by the will of the Father.

The contemplative dimension, the practice of prayer, is essential to the Christian life.

In concrete and beautiful terms Puebla invited us "to discover in the suffering faces of the poor the face of the Lord" (31-39). Santo Domingo reiterates this call and proposes that we extend further the list of those suffering faces who populate our continent (see 178 and 179). This discovery and this solidarity are the privileged way in history by which the Spirit leads us to the Father through Jesus Christ.

—*Translated by James B. Nickoloff*

CHAPTER 2

Liberating Experience: A Stimulus for European Theology

GERHARD LUDWIG MÜLLER

In my judgment, the ecclesial and theological movement that began after the Second Vatican Council in Latin America under the name "liberation theology," which has had worldwide reverberations, is one of the most significant currents of Catholic theology in the twentieth century.

If it is correct to say that Vatican II was the decisive ecclesial event in the twentieth century, then one can separate the history of contemporary theology into two phases: namely, the phase of preparation for the council that began at the end of the First World War and the phase of refinement and realization that commenced in 1965 after the council.

Regarding the phase from 1920 to 1962, one must recall the *renewal movements* that led to Vatican II: the biblical-liturgical movement, the grand blueprints of Catholic social teaching, and the renewal of our understanding of the church. These movements shaped the council and were integrated into the church's whole tradition in the conciliar documents.

After 1965, there were the various movements that the council inspired—movements that adopted the council's stimulus and orientation and that were intended to respond to the great challenges of the modern world. In this context, the greatest significance comes to liberation theology in relation to Vatican II's constitutions *Lumen gentium* and *Gaudium et spes.*

If we want to understand what changes in direction the council actually brought about, we should look not only at some of its substantive teachings but also at the new categories that originated out of the council's view of the church's origins and its mission in the world today. According to Vatican II, divine revelation is not to be understood as information about a supernatural subject matter that we obediently accept on the authority of God so that we might be rewarded after death with a heavenly blessedness. Rather, revelation is the triune God's self-communication in the incarnation of the Son and in the end-time pouring out of the Holy Spirit so that God can be known and accepted as the truth and the life of every human being and as the goal of human history.

Correspondingly, the church is not one among other religious communities that realize the ideals of its founder with more or less purity in its actions and that can be assessed in relation to an ethos of enlightened human well-being, which is praised in the contemporary paradigm of religious pluralism as "salvation-praxis." Instead, the church is the sign and instrument in Jesus Christ of God's universal saving will for all human beings. The church as the *communio* of believing people serves the human family with the Word of God, with the sacramental presentation of God's life-creating salvation, and with the demonstration of Christ's being-for-others in service of people who are poor, helpless, and deprived of their human dignity and justice.

Decisive in the council's teachings are philosophical and anthropological ideas concerning the person, dialogue, and communications. Thus, the addressee of God's self-communication is taken seriously as a person and, to be sure, as a person who is bodily embedded in history, society, and culture. In this perspective, the church—which as a community has its identity through faith in Christ and which clearly distinguishes itself from other faith-orientations and religions—does not make a totalitarian claim upon society. Rather, because of faith in Christ, the church and thus every ecclesial community and every individual Christian assume responsibility for human society as a whole in the realms of the workplace, the international economy, social and individual justice, peace in the world, and so forth.

In light of this initial, general, and entirely appreciative view of liberation theology in the history of twentieth-century theology, it is important now to explain the stimulus and transforming effects between the theologies of Latin America and Europe. Toward this goal, as a first step, I shall highlight the continuing impact of liberation theology and, as a second step, reflect on liberation theology's relation to the European context. After these thematic formulations, I will move beyond the usual comparison between the "we" in Europe and "the other" in Latin America. Rather, as a third step, I will assume a universal perspective concerning "*we* as world church" in "service *for* the world."

A New Understanding of Theology: Theological Reflection in the Service of God's Liberating Praxis

The phrase "theology of liberation" originated as the title of a lecture that Gustavo Gutiérrez gave in 1968 in Chimbote, in northern Peru. This formulation serves also as the title of his book of 1971 *Teología de la liberación: Perspectivas*.[1] This text has communicated liberation theology throughout the world. The book's revised edition of 1984 in Spanish includes a new, extensive introduction to the work.[2] Therein, Gutiérrez defines misunderstood concepts such as the preferential option for the poor, the class struggle, the

---

1. Gustavo Gutiérrez, *A Theology of Liberation: History, Politics, and Salvation*, trans. Sister Caridad Inda and John Eagleson (Maryknoll, NY: Orbis Books, 1973).

2. Gustavo Gutiérrez, *A Theology of Liberation: History, Politics, and Salvation*, trans. Sister Caridad Inda and John Eagleson, with the translation of the new introduction and revisions by Matthew J. O'Connell (Maryknoll, NY: Orbis Books, 1988).

theory of dependence, and structural or social sin. At the same time, he convincingly eviscerates the allegations of liberation theology's "horizontalism" and "immanentizing" of the Christian faith, which should never be employed as an ideological program for an earthly paradise fashioned by human beings. Distinct from the existentialist theologies of Europe, liberation theology inquires not primarily into what God, grace, and revelation contribute to the self-understanding of Christians who reside in a well-situated and socially secure middle class. Rather, it takes up the theological task of understanding and actually participating in God's comprehensive liberating action in the world, in relation to which God calls and empowers men and women to act in service for the liberation and the humanization of human beings.

It must be stressed that liberation theology is not a theoretical construct that originated at a desk. Liberation theology sees itself in continuity with the whole development of Catholic theology in the twentieth and twenty-first centuries. In view of today's new sociological structures, which have emerged out of the revolution into the modern industrial society, the globalization of markets, and the international network of all information systems, one must refer here to the social teachings of the popes, beginning with Leo XIII's encyclical *Rerum novarum* and subsequently Paul VI's *Populorum progressio*, prior to John XXIII's statement that the church must stand on the side of the poor. Out of these teachings came the comprehensive teachings and activities of Pope John Paul II.

A special source for the theology of liberation is Vatican II's Pastoral Constitution on the Church in the Modern World, *Gaudium et spes*. Previous to it, in the Dogmatic Constitution on the Church, *Lumen gentium*, the council had already presented the church not as a self-sufficient religious community standing apart from the world, but as the sacrament of the world's salvation. Along with the understanding of the church as sign and instrument working for the union of God with human beings and for the union of human beings among themselves, the church appears as servant of the salvation that God has historically constituted once and for always in

Jesus Christ and that God has made in the Holy Spirit for the continuing principle of human history and for the construction of a society befitting human beings.

On the basis of these teachings, the great synods of the Latin American bishops at Medellín (1968), Puebla (1979), and Santo Domingo (1992) understood themselves as an adaptation and concretization of the whole development of Catholic theology in the twentieth century in the social, cultural, and spiritual context of Latin America. As a result of these synods, basically all of Latin America is embracing Vatican II's new understanding of the church. Totally at odds with Vatican II's understanding of the church is the notion—which reaches back to the colonial times and is still at work even today—that the church in Latin America is comprised of a twofold division between, on the one side, a small circle of responsible people, namely, of bishops, priests, and members of religious orders who belong to the social strata of white people and have come as missionaries, and, on the other side, the passive, immature people who concern themselves only with religious rituals. These people are the indigenous people who are the descendants of the original people as well as the descendants of the black slaves and the mestizos.

Corresponding to the biblical origins and to the actual theological tradition of ecclesiology, Latin America's laity as well as its priests, catechists, and women in religious orders are increasingly seeing themselves as the bearers of the church's full mission. Among these men and women are those who were born on other continents and also those who were born in Latin America; this latter group is increasing in number and significance. The many thousand "base communities" are a living demonstration of the immediate identification of the people with the church. The church is no longer the church only for some people or only of some people; rather, the church is the people of God among the people of the earth, and thus it is the people of God for the world.

The people who are poor and disenfranchised now perceive themselves on the basis of their deep, inner encounter with the gospel; in this perspective, they are affirming their dignity as persons before God. At the same time, they are actively engaging in the life of their ecclesial community and thus fulfilling the church's mission as sacrament of the world's salvation.

Given this new self-understanding, there is also arising a new understanding of theology. Theologians are no longer presenting themselves as religious experts separate from the faithful or the nonspecialists. Rather, they understand themselves as disciples, hearing and learning from God's one Teacher and Word, namely, Christ. They are engaging in the communal experience of faith and in the people's living religiosity, that is, in the community of those who confess that Jesus is the Christ and who venture on the way of Christ's discipleship of being-for-others. In this way of life, they are participating in Christ's sufferings and hopes. Thus liberation theology, in the best sense of the word, is contextual theology that is growing out of the believing community. Thus there is also overcome the chasm between an academic university-theology, on the one hand, and, on the other, a faithful, critical reflection on the concrete experiences of the communities.

In his book *Dios o el oro en las Indias: Siglo XVI* ("God or Gold in the Indies: Sixteenth Century," 1990),[3] Gutiérrez gives an example of the path from mere theological reflection to theological reflection that matures out of a person's discipleship to Christ and in this manner into theological reflection for liberation. This book concerns the liberating way of the famous Dominican priest and later bishop Bartolomé de Las Casas, who at the beginning of the Spanish colonial time along with many other Dominican and Jesuit theologians became a champion of the human rights and the human dignity of Latin America's indigenous people. Unfortunately, it is too little known that there were Spanish theologians, such as Salamanca's Franz von Vitoria, who already two hundred years before the Enlightenment brought forth the themes of human rights and

---

3. Editor's note: Although this book has not appeared in English, it was incorporated in the much-expanded work *Las Casas: In Search of the God of Jesus Christ* (Maryknoll, NY: Orbis Books, 1993).

tribal rights as well as the critique of the legalized disenfranchising of Latin America's original people.

The theology of liberation does not refer to a new divine revelation. It intends only to be a new method of presenting Christians' collaboration in God's world-changing praxis. In this regard, Gutiérrez gives a definition of liberation theology:

> Theology as critical reflection on historical praxis is a liberating theology, a theology of the liberating transformation of the history of humankind and also therefore that part of humankind—gathered into *ecclesia*—which openly confesses Christ. This is a theology which does not stop with reflecting on the world, but rather tries to be part of the process through which the world is transformed. It is a theology which is open—in the protest against trampled human dignity, in the struggle against the plunder of the vast majority of humankind, in liberating love, and in the building of a new, just, and comradely society—to the gift of the Kingdom of God.[4]

It should be stressed that "salvation" and "liberation" are synonyms for the encompassing, holistic encounter of human beings with God who in Jesus Christ has entered into communion with suffering humanity in need of salvation. In his reflection on liberation, Gutiérrez differentiates sin in relation to *three* levels: on its first level, sin is the innermost rupture of the friendship between God and human beings, and the sin of this first level is the root of all forms of a human being's inner and outer enslavement. This rupture shows itself in a second level as we seek to loosen ourselves from the inner slavery to the powers of unreflective profit-seeking. Further, the rupture between God and human beings shows itself in a third level as we in discipleship to Christ try to overcome the oppression and marginalization within which exploitation and murderous economic and social abuses express themselves. This third level is social and structural sin, and it is a manifestation of the second level, personal sin.

---

4. Gutiérrez, *A Theology of Liberation* (2014) 12.

In this context, we should distinguish between poverty and hunger. In a biblical perspective, "poverty" [in the sense of "hunger"] means the misery that deprives human beings of dignity; it characterizes the universal necessity of human beings for salvation, the human beings to whom gospel is proclaimed. "Poverty" can also mean the spiritual openness to and availability for service for the kingdom of God. The poverty that the gospel calls for does not mean that Christians should freely give themselves over to situations that deprive them of their human dignity. When men and women who are members of a religious congregation praise poverty, they are renouncing personal property in order to share entirely through prayer and work in the mission of their religious community, for example, in the service of human beings who are sick or impoverished or in the service of education and personal formation in schools and at universities. With this distinction in mind, we can understand the well-known formulation of Pope John Paul II who, in a letter to the Brazilian bishops, underscored the necessity of the theology of liberation.[5] The pope himself was inspired by the theology of liberation. When he was speaking at the Villa El Salvador (which stands in a poor district to the south of Lima, Peru), he declared to millions of people: "The hunger for bread must disappear; the hunger for God will remain."[6]

The theology of liberation is not a religiously clothed sociology or a type of socio-theology. Liberation theology is theology in the strict sense.

Fundamental is the belief that God has created human beings in God's image, and also the belief that God is personally active in his Son Jesus Christ for human beings, even when Jesus accepted the death to which his opponents condemned him. The goal of liberation theology is make discernible in all dimensions of human life that God is the God of life and the conqueror of death. Liberation

---

5. See Gutiérrez, *A Theology of Liberation* (2014) xliv.

6. See Gustavo Gutiérrez, "Gustavo Gutiérrez im Gespräch mit Josef Sayer," in Peter Eicher, ed., *Theologie der Befreiung im Gespräch* (Munich: Kösel Verlag, 1985) 46.

theology overcomes all dualisms that want to exile God to the "other side" and God's salvation to an interior realm [apart from history].

Every human being stands in the inner tension between the proclaimed being of God in creation and salvation history, on the one hand, and, on the other, the anticipated fulfillment beyond the boundaries of individual death and the universal end of history. According to liberation theology, Christian belief demands our participation through our understanding of and our acting in the process of God's transformation of history, which God has definitively inaugurated in the saving action of Jesus Christ as the movement toward God. There is no talk here of the primacy of orthopraxis over orthodoxy. When something is said about the primacy of praxis, there is intended no reduction of Christian belief to ethics. Rather, the emphasis is on our participation in the praxis of God in love, which can be recognized only through faith in the Word of God's self-revelation.

Given this orientation, liberation theology relies on a method of three steps.

First, in faith Christians actively participate through discipleship to Jesus in God's praxis for the liberation of human beings and for their personal dignity and their salvation.

In its analysis of society, liberation theology employs the methods of the human and social sciences, and [with this inductive starting point] it distinguishes itself from classical theology, which has philosophy alone as its dialogue partner. The critical questions of the Congregation for the Doctrine of the Faith (CDF) in its Instruction on Christian Freedom and Liberation, *Libertatis nuntius* (1984), have their justification insofar as they are a reminder of the necessity of differentiating between the data generated by the social sciences and the ideological reductionisms that often appeal to this data. When the empirical anthropologies are clarified in the light of a philosophical and theological anthropology, they are made fruitful for the posing of theological questions.

As is well known, liberation theology in a comprehensive sense is valued in the CDF's second clarification, its Instruction on Certain

Aspects of the Theology of Liberation, *Libertatis conscientia* (1986). Similarly, Pope John Paul II's encyclical *Fides et ratio* (1998) has established with full vigor that theology is concerned not only with a faith-filled exposition of Christian texts. Rather, when theology engages in a dialogue with philosophy and also with the human and social sciences, it can fulfill its service on behalf of the truth about human beings in the horizon of their relationship with God.

As the *second* methodological step, there occurs the critical and rational analysis—undertaken in light of the gospel and divine revelation—of society, in particular, concerning the national and international causes of extensive poverty as well as this poverty's historical and structural dimensions.

Finally, the *third* step leads from critical reflection to action for the transformation of the empirical state of affairs. The goal is God's lordship on earth, as Jesus proclaimed it. In this regard, one must understand God's lordship as a dynamic principle that serves as the driving force in the concrete situations of the people who are suffering because of individual factors and social structures for human life, flawed structures that are the result of our alienation from God.

This theological orientation includes the preferential option for those who are poor and deprived of their human dignity. However, this option for the poor does not exclude people who are wealthy; these people, too, are the intended recipients of God's liberating action. God's liberating action is meant to free people from their anxieties, especially from those irrational concerns that impel them to seize life for themselves at the expense of other people. God's liberating action both toward the poor and also toward the rich has the same aim: God seeks to bring about each human being's development into a personal subject and thus into freedom from every form of oppression and dependence.

That salvation is to be understood as liberating action shows itself in the Old Testament in the experience of the exodus. God releases the enslaved Israelites not to something better beyond this life. Rather, God leads them to the land of promise, which is the land of freedom.

God's liberating action culminates in the Christ event. Jesus proclaimed God's lordship as the gospel for the people who are poor, cast out, and sick. Jesus demonstrated the liberating action of God in relation to the opposition of sinners, including when he demonstrated the love of God in his own death as the basis of human existence in life and death. Through Jesus' cross and death God qualifies the world as the realm of the ongoing, new creation. The cross is the revelation of God's option for the people who are suffering, deprived of their rights, tortured, and murdered. In Jesus' resurrection from the dead, God has shown all people in an original and exemplary manner what life truly is and how freedom can transpose itself into an empowering existence for people and into a struggle for the living conditions appropriate to human dignity.

One can characterize the theology of liberation's essential fruit in Gustavo Gutiérrez's words:

> If theological reflection does not vitalize the action of the Christian community in the world by making its commitment to charity fuller and more radical, if—more concretely—in Latin America it does not lead the Church to be on the side of the oppressed classes and dominated peoples, clearly and without qualifications, then this theological reflection will have been of little value. Worse yet, it will have served only to justify half-measures and ineffective approaches and to rationalize a departure from the Gospel.
>
> We must be careful not to fall into an intellectual self-satisfaction, into a kind of triumphalism of erudite and advanced "new" visions of Christianity. The only thing that is really new is to accept day by day the gift of the Spirit, who makes us love—in our concrete options to build a true human fellowship, in our historical initiatives to subvert an order of injustice—with the fullness with which Christ loved us. To paraphrase a well-known text of Pascal, we can say that all the political theologies, the theologies of hope, of revolution, and of liberation, are not worth one act of genuine solidarity with exploited social classes. They are not worth one act of faith,

love, and hope, committed—in one way or another—in active participation to liberate humankind from everything that dehumanizes it and prevents it from living according to the will of the Father.[7]

*Liberation Theology in the Energy Field
between Latin America and Europe*

During the 1970s and 1980s, the theology of liberation evoked a great resonance in Europe. Above all, the interest of young Christians for Latin America increased enormously. Amid the change of consciousness during the student revolution of 1968 with its critique of the bourgeois-capitalist mentality of well-being, the liberation theology of Latin America was received in Europe as a reinforcement of a political theology. The church's prophetic service in society and the gospel's transformative power in relation to the structures of dependence, exploitation, and the misuse of power were set against a religious interiority that had been reduced to a private, inner realm. The European opponents of the call for a transformation of society spoke about liberation theology's "immanentizing" of faith and also about its confusion of theological views with a neo-Marxist analysis of society.

After the fall of the Berlin Wall in 1989 and the collapse of the communist-governed Eastern Bloc in 1991 it appeared to many observers to be only a matter of time until Latin America would have to give up its opposition to and protest against centuries of exploitation and disenfranchisement, first by the colonial powers and then by the North American and European business centers. This protest was seen as coming to expression in the theology of liberation. The notion of the so-called "naturally determined" division of roles between the rich lands and the poor lands appeared to be on the upswing. The virus of Marxism was to blame—it was said— for the occasions when men and women had abruptly set them-

---

7. Gutiérrez, *A Theology of Liberation* (2014) 174.

selves against their being taken advantage of as a cheap labor force and against the exporting of their land's raw materials for a trifling price in exchange for national defense. This allegation of a Marxist influence also occurred when people no longer relinquished their desire for basic medical care, for a civil government oriented toward human rights and legal protections, for formal education, and for housing appropriate to human dignity.

Mixed into the triumphalism of a supposedly victorious capitalism was a dark delight, a *Schadenfreude*, that the theology of liberation had apparently lost its underpinning. Some people believed that they had won an easy game against this theology, which they associated with revolutionary power and with the terrorism of Marxist groups.

In its notorious secret document of 1980 for President Reagan, the Committee of Santa Fe called upon the U.S. government to act offensively against the theology of liberation and the Catholic Church of Latin America influenced by this theology. This document declares: "The role of the church in Latin America is of vital significance for political freedom. Unfortunately, the Marxist-Leninist powers have used the church as a political weapon against private property and the capitalist system of production; they have infiltrated the religious community with ideas which are less Christian and much more communist."[8] Alarming in this document is the insensitivity with which the representatives of brutal military dictators and powerful oligarchies—the representatives responsible for this document—make their interest in private property and capitalist production into the criterion for what is to be valued as Christian.

It must be clarified that the private property to which this document refers is not the meager-paying, small parcels of land but the property of the giant estates and of the copper and silver mines in which millions of small farmers and workers, lacking possessions and rights, barely survive. Moreover, the background to this document includes the political, financially sponsored, activities of fun-

---

8. Quoted in Eicher, ed., *Theologie des Befreiung im Gespräch*, 40-41.

damentalist Christian sects. The struggle of liberation theology for a comprehensive view of grace and salvation is pushed away since these sects see the role of religion to be to give an other-worldly, vague promise and an interior disposition, and thus religion is misused as a stabilizing element in a socially unjust society.

The document's proponents manifest contempt for human beings. Most offensive are the specific North American institutions that make their shipments of food and aid for Peru contingent on a dramatic decline in the nation's birth rate. The Peruvian government acted on this demand when, under the pretext of health examinations, it either injected men and women with drugs to prevent conceptions or had people sterilized, and it did all of this without the knowledge of the people and against their consciences. Here the slogan appears to be: Struggle against poverty by decimating the people who are poor. When someone presupposes that a high birthrate is the cause of misery, one becomes diverted from poverty's true causes. Talk about overpopulation in Peru rings hollow in light of the fact that this nation is five times greater in geographical size than Germany but has five times fewer people than Germany. Anyone who perceives, simply on the basis of his or her own observations, the millions of ways in which the Peruvian people are devalued, enslaved, and exploited will hardly be convinced by talk that praises the efficiency and superiority of capitalism.

In order to avoid a misunderstanding, a clarification of the meaning of "capitalism" is indispensable. In the Latin American context the word capitalism connotes the human striving without limits for a personal empire. Indeed, this striving is raised to the sole principle of human action. This kind of capitalism has nothing to do with a free-enterprise system in which men and women contribute their work and abilities in a social, free-market economy that functions within a democratically constructed legal system.

In light of the failure of the pure capitalist system and of the mentality of human disdain that belongs to it, liberation theology sticks with an immediate state of affairs. What basically differentiates the theology of liberation from Marxism and also from capitalism is exactly what binds together these two economic systems, despite all of their differences. That is, both systems hold an understanding of human beings and a notion of society in which God, Jesus Christ, and the gospel play no role in the humanization of a human being as an individual or as the member of a community. Communism always runs aground because it rests on a deficient anthropology: it neither evaluates a human being in the ideal nor does it overlook the innate egoism of a human being. However, it has also overlooked the orientation of a human being to God, and thus it has kept silent about the reality of sin and grace, about forgiveness and a possible life on the basis of God's given justice.

At the same time, unbridled capitalism also runs aground because it too rests on the same deficient anthropology in the sense that one can define a human being without God and can construct a society without recourse to God's Word and grace. If someone understands capitalism as a market economy determined not by justice and human dignity but by an anthropology concerning the rights of the people who are stronger, then one must reject the claim that democracy functions well only on the requirements of capitalism.

Democracy in the modern sense relies not solely on the will of the majority or on the unexamined presupposition of the rights of an individual. Rather, democracy is rooted in an act of acknowledgment of human rights, an acknowledgment that prohibits every form of government and economic manipulation. Thus modern democracy has its roots and the guarantee of its existence in an act of faith in a Higher Power, before which the human being is responsible for his or her relationships with one's neighbors. For this reason, liberation theology is a basic democratic activity and a defender of human rights against threats either from the totalitarian, Marxist ideologies or from the "neoliberal," capitalist ideologies, both of which threaten Latin America and Europe.[9]

---

9. Translator's note: The "neoliberal" economic theory, developed by Milton Friedman (d. 2006) and the Chicago school of economics, values a free market system with little or no government intervention. Espoused by President Ronald Reagan, it is endorsed by neoconservative politicians in the United States.

Liberation theology will not die as long as there are men and women who are motivated by God's liberating action and pursue—by the measure of their faith and by the drive of their social action—their solidarity with their neighbors who are suffering, their neighbors whose dignity has been tossed into the trash. To put it succinctly, liberation theology involves believing in God as a God of life and guarantor of a holistically understood salvation of the human being and also as acting in opposition to the gods who desire the premature death, poverty, impoverishment, and devaluation of human beings.

As Gutiérrez frequently points out, liberation theology is often misunderstood by its advocates and its opponents, both of whom hold that the liberation theologians are primarily interested in the social and political dimensions of human life, and, in this, they work somewhat amateurishly in areas, such as economics, politics, and sociology, that are unfamiliar to them. It is alleged that amid this approach these theologians lose sight of theology's proper theme, namely, the fundamental relationship of the human being to God. However, on the contrary, whoever takes the starting point of liberation theology seriously marvels at its strictly theocentric and christocentric starting point as well as at its integration into the living community of the church.

Liberation theologians are similar to Dietrich Bonhoeffer, who in the context of Europe's secularization discovered that nonbelievers are the appropriate dialogue partners for Christian theology, and thus he asked, "How can someone *speak about God* in a world that has come of age?" Similarly, in light of the fact that the majority of people in Latin America are Christian, Gustavo Gutiérrez views these Christians as theology's dialogue partners, and thus he asks, "How can someone *speak about God* in light of the suffering, premature death, and poverty of Latin America's people who are deprived of their personal dignity?"

The attempt to bring about a genuine integration of talk about God and of concrete encouragement for the people who are awaiting God's salvation was previously pursued by authors such as

Maurice Blondel, Henri de Lubac, Juan Alfaro, and Karl Rahner—all of whom were important for the genesis of liberation theology. These theologians contributed (in the mid-twentieth century) to an energetic discussion concerning the relationship between nature and grace, and this discussion was decisive for an entirely new understanding of Christian belief's relationship to the secular and autonomous view of the human being that was generated by the European Enlightenment and modernity.

The question at the heart of the discussion was this: are there two parallel orders—a secular-autonomous determination of a human being and a supernatural revelation—so that a human being exists in two spheres of thought and life that are completely separate from each other? Or, is a human being in his or her inner personal unity and center addressed by God and called to a religious and ethical unity of personal and social life?

At the starting point of a theological response, there is the understanding of divine revelation as the synthesis of the liberation of human beings by God and as the collaboration of human beings in the liberating and salvific action of God. As a result, there is an inseparable, unifying relation between creation and salvation, faith and the world order, the appeal of transcendence and the orientation to immanence, history and eschatology, the spiritual relationship to Christ and the identification with Christ in a life of discipleship. Liberation theology leads therefore beyond the inflexible scheme of a dualism between "this world" and "that world," a dualism in which religion is thoroughly reduced to an individual human being's mystical experience. In such a dualistic view, religiosity has the function of motivating someone toward an individual morality or to a social ethic.

As a central perspective, the "preferential option for the poor"—which originated out of the praxis and experience of Latin America's Christian communities—has profoundly shaped the church in Latin America. Service for liberating praxis realizes itself in the horizon of a theocentric view of a human being and of God's encouragement, directed to the human being, for enabling the salvation of the human being. Concerning this orientation of the Latin American church, Gutiérrez writes:

> All of this means that an entirely new epoch is beginning. Ever more clearly there is the necessity of a competition to pick out from the options the best possible solution for Latin America's enormous problems. There is available a restoration of the social structure in which at one time we sought the starting point for the proclamation of the reign of God. The new situation demands new methods of a liberating praxis. Here it is of importance to be attentive and not to go backwards, not to go either toward a "verticalism of a spiritual union with God without ties to our human bodies, or toward a simple existentialist personalism of an individual or a small group and also not toward a horizontalism of a social, economic, and political kind."[10]

> Both extremes (of verticalism and horizontalism) push every person from his or her true unity and simultaneously against the transcendence and the immanence of the Kingdom of God insofar as these two dimensions cannot be separated from each other.[11]

A New Sense of "We" in the Church and in the Service of the Salvation of Others

From the sixteenth century into the twentieth century, the relationship between Latin America and Europe was shaped by the meeting, or perhaps the collision, of religious cultures. Today in Europe, after the advance of the Enlightenment with its critique of religion

---

10. Gustavo Gutiérrez is quoting from the concluding document of the Third General Conference of Latin American Bishops in Puebla, Mexico (CELAM III). This document is "The Evangelization of Latin America in the Present and the Future" (February 19, 1979).

11. See this book's first chapter: Gustavo Gutiérrez, "Theology: An Ecclesial Function," p. 1.

and its secularization of society, the expectation of now uniting in European society the previous Christian culture and Christian faith has declined among a great many people. Similarly, in Latin America there is no longer the effort to bring together culture and faith. Moreover, at this time, the existence of business networks, global market strategies, and concurring religious and ideological systems of meaning in the pluralistic world society mean that it no longer makes sense to contrast a European collective subject, a "we," and a Latin American "we." In fact, when there is talk about "We in Europe . . . ," it is appropriate to ask, "To which 'we' does this talk refer?"

Further, the church has sought since Vatican II to translate its Catholicity into tangible realities for today's people, and it has defined anew its mission as sacrament of the world's salvation. In this situation, one may ask, is the "we" determined by anything more than region and culture? In the different parts of the world, one can experience that Christians are defining their Christian identity by their belonging to Christ and no longer in some roundabout way in relation to Europe's Christian-shaped culture. As a result, experiences of the church's "we" can vary from one region of the world to another. Also, European Christians perceive that their roots are grounded in "Western Christian culture," which itself is not monolithic but highly differentiated. At the same time, they define themselves on the basis of their faith in Christ. Through this personal connection to Christ, they discover the "we" of the church and their ties to many people around the world. Indeed, in their orientation to Christ, European Christians accept the church's "we" as constitutive for their faith.

Further, we in Europe have moved beyond forms of colonialism that combine religious gestures and capitalistic exploitation. At this point, it does not suffice for us to acknowledge and regret our former Euro-centrism, paternalism, and assistance mentality. Our self-accusation cannot be the last word concerning the relationship between Europe and Latin America. We must seek an entirely new way forward for the twenty-first century. The one-sidedness of the past will not be overcome if we emphasize only a relationship of reciprocal giving and taking, of teaching and learning. Rather, we must strive for the recognition that the people around the world who believe in Christ form the one "we" of his church, and that, guided by this faith perspective, the world church must realize itself in a reciprocal exchange within the global community of local churches. This theologically defined unity of all believers in the *communio* of the local churches will enable the church to address the great challenges of the modern world and to make its specific contribution to the forming of the world society on the basis of individual and social human rights.

This newly determined relationship of the church to the contemporary world was envisioned in the unsurpassable statement of *Gaudium et spes*, article 1:

> The joys and hopes, the grief and anguish of the people of our time, especially of those who are poor or afflicted, are the joys and hopes, the grief and anguish of the followers of Christ as well. Nothing that is genuinely human fails to find an echo in their hearts. For theirs is a community of people united in Christ and guided by the Holy Spirit in their pilgrimage towards the Father's kingdom, bearers of a message of salvation for all of humanity. That is why they cherish a feeling of deep solidarity with the human race and its history.[12]

Liberation theology can insert its essential stimulus into this new "we" of the worldwide, one church in relation to humanity in its search for a sense, going beyond the finite world, of the existence of God and simultaneously in its responsibility for earthly life.

Standing with Gustavo Gutiérrez, we can sum up the continuing influence of liberation theology in the elements that we as the church can learn for the world today. In particular, Gutiérrez has pinpointed three themes in light of the Latin American bish-

---

12. Austin Flannery, O.P., ed., *Vatican Council II: The Basic Sixteen Documents. A Completely Revised Translation in Inclusive Language* (Northport, NY: Costello Publishing Company, 1996) 163.

ops' meeting in Santo Domingo in 1992.[13] These three themes are urgent not only for the people of Latin America but also for people in Europe as well: new evangelization, human progress, and the inculturation of the gospel.[14] Concerning these themes, consider Gutiérrez's statement which extends for several pages in his essay "Theology: An Ecclesial Function."[15]

New evangelization, the church's service for a social and just society, and a new synthesis of the Christian faith and modern culture are the greatest challenges facing the church in Europe.

—Translated by Robert A. Krieg

---

13. Translator's note: The Fourth General Conference of Latin American Bishops, CELAM IV, was held in Santo Domingo, Dominican Republic, from October 12 to October 28, 1992. On October 12, Pope John Paul II gave the conference's opening address.

14. Translator's note: CELAM IV's concluding document is "New Evangelization, Human Promotion, and Christian Culture" (January 22, 1993).

15. Editor's note: Müller here quotes several pages taken from Gutiérrez's essay, which appears as chap. 1 in this volume; see pp. 8-10.

CHAPTER 3

The Situation and Tasks
of Liberation Theology Today

GUSTAVO GUTIÉRREZ

The question that has been put to me concerns the future of liberation theology. Two clarifications are necessary before beginning to
make several points on this subject.

Efforts to understand faith, which we call theologies, are closely
linked to questions that come from life and from the challenges that
the Christian community faces in bearing witness to the reign of
God. Thus theology is connected to the historical moment and cultural world in which these questions arise (thus, to say that a theology is "contextual" is, strictly speaking, tautological; in one way or
another every theology is contextual). This is one of the elements
that establish theology as an ecclesial duty. Obviously, there are permanent elements in theologies that come from the Christian message, which is their focus; theologies help us to see these elements in
a new light. But a theology's relevance depends in large part on its
capacity to interpret the form in which faith is lived in a particular
time and circumstances. The consequence is clear: on their mutable
side, theologies are born in a precise framework and contribute (or
should contribute) to the faith-life of believers and to the evangelizing task of the church, but the accents, categories, terms, and focal
points lose their "bite" to the extent that the situation that gave rise
to them is no longer the same. What I am saying about the historicity of every theology, including those that endured longest in the
course of Christianity's history, is obviously true for an endeavor

such as that of liberation theology. Theology always sinks its roots in the historical density of the gospel message.[1]

This leads me to a second observation, which complements the preceding one. What matters more than wondering about the future of a theology as such is to ask about the relevance and consequences of the great themes of Christian revelation which that theology has been able to revitalize and fix in the consciousness of believers. In the case of a faith-understanding reached through the lens of liberation, this would involve such points as the liberation process (with all the dimensions that this implies) of the poor in Latin America, the presence of the gospel and of Christians on this journey, and, in a very special way, the preferential option for the poor put forward and developed in this kind of theological reflection. These are situations and themes in continuous evolution. This is what really counts.

Perhaps a good way to consider the future of a theological perspective would be to set it over against other theological orientations of today, to submit its aim and its central axes to a new examination in relation to the present moment, and then to take a look at the tasks that it faces. In fact, the future does not simply arrive; we build it. We make it with our hands and hopes, our failures and plans, our stubbornness and our sensitivity to what is new. This is what I propose to present schematically in three steps in the pages that follow.

Three Great Contemporary Challenges to Faith

In convoking the Second Vatican Council John XXIII asked us—and himself—how to say today what Christians pray for

---

1. This is why—curiously enough—those who wonder if liberation theology remains valid after the events symbolized by the fall of the Berlin Wall (certainly an event of enormous importance on the international stage) need to be reminded that the historical starting point for this theology was not the situation of the Eastern European countries. It was, and certainly continues to be, the inhuman poverty of Latin America and the interpretation we make of it in the light of faith. What we have, then, is a state of things and a theology that, at their core, have little to do with the collapse of real socialism.

daily, namely, that "your kingdom come." In seeking an answer to this prayer, he recovered an important biblical theme: the need to know how to discern the signs of the times. This means being attentive to the movement of history and, more broadly, to the world in which we live out our faith. It means being sensitive to the questions that the world raises, questions that challenge us and enrich us at the same time. Thus it also means being far from fears, from condemnations at all costs, and from the narrow-mindedness of those whom the same pope called "prophets of doom"—an attitude so relished by those who set themselves up as saviors from all the evils of the age.

In this order of ideas we could say, without making any exhaustive claim and leaving aside important nuances, that Christian faith and the proclamation of the gospel today face three great challenges: (1) the modern world and what is called postmodernity, (2) the poverty of so many, and (3) religious pluralism and the interreligious dialogue it requires. The three make far-reaching demands on Christian life and on the church's work. At the same time all three furnish elements and categories that allow us to take new paths in understanding and deepening the Christian message. It is essential to take these two facets of a single reality into account. Theological work will consist of confronting, face-to-face, these challenges that stand before it as signs of the times. At the same time, we must discern in them—in the light of faith—the new hermeneutical field that they offer us for reflecting on our faith and for speaking about a God who talks to the people of our time.

I would like to dedicate the greater part of these pages to the second of these challenges. Let us, then, examine the first and third more briefly.

The Modern (and Postmodern) World

With roots in the fifteenth and sixteenth centuries, the mentality that would come to be called "modern" had an effect on the life of the Christian churches from the eighteenth century on. It is characterized by (a) the affirmation of the individual as the starting point for economic activity, social life, and human knowledge; (b) critical reason, which accepts only what has been subjected to the examination and judgment of reason itself; and (c) the right to freedom in various spheres. It is what Kant called humanity's coming of age. This is what gives rise to the modern spirit's distrust of authority, on both the social and the religious plane. Christian faith, close to superstition and of an authoritarian bent—according to this line of thought—was destined to disappear or at best to be confined to the private sphere. In this way society would enter a rapid process of secularization and would make Christian faith lose the social weight and influence over people that it had in other times.[2] The forms this conflict took, for European Christians in a particular way, are well known. Also well known are the steps taken, and the steps not taken, in the responses provoked by these different disputes with the church. And this is to say nothing of the uncertainty, fear, effrontery, and suffering that people lived through for these reasons.

Vatican II distanced itself from those who saw nothing more in the modern world than a bad period destined to pass and who thought the only thing to do was to steadfastly resist until the storm dissipated. The council searched for and succeeded in finding answers to many of these questions (though not without difficulties and misunderstandings at the beginning, of course). There is still an enormous amount of work to do in relation to the situation created by modernity. It is clear that in this matter we face a long process.[3]

The task has become more complicated in recent years because of what has come to be called, for convenience, the postmodern

---

2. One of the important factors in this process was, as we know, scientific thought. The matter has acquired a new urgency with the development of aspects of science (biogenetics, for example) that raise serious questions for the Christian view of life.

3. See in this regard the important work *Historia del Concilio Vatican II* in process of publication in various languages, directed by Giuseppe Alberigo.

era.[4] The postmodern outlook presents itself as a sharp criticism of modernity, which it accuses, among other things, of drifting into totalitarianism (fascism, Nazism, and Stalinism), thus contradicting its fervent assertion of liberty and of confining itself to a narrow and purely instrumental view of reason. Postmodernity sharpens the individualism that characterizes the modern world. The result of all this has been a somewhat apathetic stance toward possibilities for changing what used to be seen as not functioning well in our societies. The same can be said of its distrust of solid convictions in any area of human action or knowledge; thus there arises a skeptical stance that relativizes the knowledge of truth. According to this view, we all have our own truth, and thus everything is valid. This stance is without doubt one of the reasons for the lack of interest in social and political reality that we see in our time. This mentality, of course, also makes important contributions: from now on we will have to pay attention, for example, to what our assessment of cultural or ethnic diversity (with all its political ambivalences) might mean.

Whether postmodernity is a rejection of modernity or a more refined prolongation of it does not change the essence of what concerns me here. Taken as a whole, postmodernity constitutes a great challenge to Christian consciousness. The passage of time, it is true, has brought about valuable theological works that have taken the bull by the horns. Far from being a repudiation inspired by fear, they have not only faced the questions posed by the modern world and its repercussions with evangelical freedom and fidelity to the message of Jesus; these works have also pointed out what the modern world itself could contribute so that the significance of faith might be revealed to those to whom we had not been sensitive in the past or who, for one reason or another, had been eclipsed in the course of history.

---

4. See Gustavo Gutiérrez, "¿Dónde dormirán los pobres?" in *El rostro de Dios en la historia* (Lima: Universidad Católica, Instituto Bartolomé de Las Casas, CEP, 1996) 9-69.

Religious Pluralism

The great number of religions is, as we know, a very ancient fact of the human race. While both the great and well-known religions, as well as the less-widespread ones, were not created yesterday, the contemporary problematic in this regard has reached theological consciousness only in recent years. In the past, religious pluralism raised certain practical problems and led to a consideration of the salvific potential of the missionary task of Christian churches, but in recent decades its presence has become a question of great magnitude for Christian faith. All those who study this topic agree that a theology of world religions, such as we find it today, is very recent and is moving along a path strewn with difficulties. Today we see a great debate about this taking place in the church. The question is, of course, delicate, and important texts from the magisterium, as well as inspiring theological studies, have been devoted to it.[5] As in the case of the modern world, but for different reasons, the existence of billions of human beings who find in these religions their relationship to God or to an Absolute or to the deepest meaning of their lives raises questions about fundamental points of Christian theology. At the same time, as also happens in the case of modernity, this fact furnishes elements and possibilities for theology to take another look at itself and to examine the meaning and significance today of salvation in Jesus Christ.

This is new and demanding territory.[6] Here there is a great temptation to withdraw and stick to positions considered safe. For this reason bold gestures such as those of John Paul II are particularly welcome; I am thinking of the invitation he issued a few years ago to representatives of the great religions of humanity to meet in Assisi to pray for the peace of the world. In fact, a theology of world religions cannot be constructed apart from the practice of interre-

---

5. See, for example, Jacques Dupuis, *Vers une théologie chrétienne du pluralisme religieux* (Paris: Cerf, 1997).

6. For a brief overview, the reader may consult M. Fédou, *Les religions selon la foi chrétienne* (Paris: Cerf, 1996).

ligious dialogue, a dialogue that up to now has barely begun. Theology is always a second act. Many people are involved in this effort, and here too, and perhaps with greater urgency than in the previous challenge, there is an enormous amount of work to be done.

The modern mentality is the fruit of important changes in the field of human knowledge and in social life. These changes took place primarily in Western Europe when it had already begun its march to a standard of living that would distance it from the rest of the planet's countries. By contrast, those who bring questions arising from religious pluralism are found among the poorest nations of humanity. Perhaps this is one of the reasons why, as I noted, awareness of the questions they pose has only very recently arisen in the Christian churches, precisely at the time when these peoples were starting to make their voices heard in different regions of the world. This means that the response to the questions coming from Asia above all, but also from Africa and to a lesser degree from Latin America, must not separate religious matters from the situation of poverty. This twofold reality has many consequences for the faith-discourse coming from these regions.[7]

This last observation leads me to take up the challenge that comes from poverty. I will treat it at greater length, as it is a matter that is of particular concern to me.

An Inhuman and Anti-evangelical Poverty

The challenges to Christian faith that come from religious pluralism and from poverty were born outside the North Atlantic world. Those who bear them on their shoulders are the poor peoples of humanity, as I just said in regard to the world religions, and this is obviously the case with poverty. This final challenge to theological reflection was first raised with intensity in Latin America, a conti-

---

7. This is a point on which Sri Lankan theologian Aloysius Pieris rightly insists. See, for example, *An Asian Theology of Liberation* (Maryknoll, NY: Orbis Books, 1988).

nent whose population is simultaneously *poor and believing*, as we have been saying for decades in the framework of liberation theology. I am referring to those who live out their faith in the midst of poverty, which means that each of these characteristics leaves its mark on the other; to live out and think through Christian faith cannot therefore be accomplished apart from an awareness of the situation of exploitation and marginalization in which such persons find themselves.

Rereading the Message

The Latin American bishops' meetings held in Medellín (1968) and Puebla (1979) denounced the continent's poverty as "inhuman" and "anti-evangelical." But unfortunately we know that this is a worldwide phenomenon. Little by little the poor of the world were gaining a clearer awareness of their situation. A series of historical events in the 1950s and 1960s (decolonization, new nations, popular movements, a better understanding of the causes of poverty, etc.) made present around the globe those who had always been *absent* from the history of humanity or, to be more exact, invisible to those who limit history to the deeds of one part of it—the Western world—which is made to appear as the winner in every field. The historical fact that has been called the "irruption of the poor" is not, of course, an event that is finished; it is still in full swing and continues to raise new and pertinent questions. In Latin America and in the Caribbean this event was, and is, of particular significance for theological reflection.

Poverty is, like the religious pluralism of humanity, a situation that has existed for a long time. In the past it certainly led to admirable demonstrations of service to the poor and abandoned. But today knowledge of its crushing extent, the ever wider and deeper gap between the rich and the poor in contemporary society, and the way we have of conceiving it have meant that only in the second half of the century just ended has it really been seen as a challenge to our understanding of faith. Even now this is not true everywhere because there are still those for whom poverty remains only a problem of the social and economic order. This is not the biblical meaning of poverty, nor was it John XXIII's view when, on the eve of the council, he placed the church face to face with the poverty of the world ("the underdeveloped countries") and affirmed that it had to be "the church of all and especially the church of the poor." He thus proposed a demanding way of conceiving the church and its task in the world.

The message of Pope John was heard and later deepened in Latin America and the Caribbean: being a continent that is both poor and at the same time Christian, as I mentioned above, made us particularly sensitive to the theological depth of the challenge raised by poverty. This is a perspective that, in the different circumstances of the sixteenth century, figures such as Bartolomé de Las Casas and Peruvian Indian Guaman Poma pioneered in these lands in their defense of the indigenous population of the continent. Even today it is still far from being understood by everyone. This is why we still have problems trying to make clear the meaning of the basic affirmations of liberation theology and of the bishops' conference of Medellín, both of which, taking into account the present context, have a bearing precisely on our approach.

Despite this, the church of Latin America and the Caribbean and, soon after, the churches of other poor continents made clear just how far the demands go that arise from the situation of poverty and the marginalization of so many human beings. This issue is still pushing forward amid certain obstacles, so that it can be seen in its true depth as a problem for Christian life and theological reflection. It is important to note that this happens less with the challenge concerning the role of the world religions in the saving plan of the God of Christian revelation. In the case of religious pluralism, although there are those who refuse to go along, the theological character of the problem is seen, of course, more quickly. To underline the theological character of the questions that poverty brings does not in any way mean to dodge the unavoidable and constitutive socioeconomic dimension that poverty and social injustice have. This is obviously the case. But the attention that should be given to poverty and social injustice does not come merely from a concern with social and political problems. Poverty as it is known to us today hurls a radical and all-encompassing question at the human conscience and at the way we perceive Christian faith. It constitutes a hermeneutical field that leads us to a rereading of the biblical message and of the path we should take as disciples of Jesus. This is something that should be stressed if we want to understand the meaning of a theology such as the theology of liberation.

An Axis of Christian Life

What I have just said is captured quite clearly in the well-known expression "preferential option for the poor." The term arose in the Christian communities and in the theological reflections of Latin America in the time between Medellín and Puebla. The latter conference took it up and made it known far and wide. Its roots lie in the experiences of solidarity with the poor and in the corresponding understanding of the biblical meaning of poverty, which had their beginnings early in the 1960s and which had already been expressed—at least the heart of the matter—at Medellín. This expression is very common today in the teachings of John Paul II and of different episcopal conferences of the universal church, as well as in the documents of various Christian denominations. The preferential option for the poor person is a fundamental axis in the proclamation of the gospel, which we commonly call (using the well-known biblical metaphor) the pastoral task. It is also a fundamental axis in the field of spirituality, that is, in the following of Jesus. Thus it is likewise an axis in our attempt to make sense of the faith, which is done by beginning with these two dimensions of the Christian life. Taken as a whole, this threefold character is what gives it strength and scope.

I have just traced the short history of a perception that is expressed in the formula noted: nevertheless, it is clear that at its core this formula is intended to help us see how in this age we approach a central datum of biblical revelation that in one way or another has always been part of the Christian universe. I am referring to God's love for every person and particularly for those who are most abandoned. But it happens that today we are in a position to be able to point out with all the clarity one could wish that the poverty, injustice, and marginalization of persons and of groups of persons are not irrevocable facts, but they have human and social causes. Furthermore, we are shocked by the immensity of this reality and by the growing distance, from this point of view, between the nations of the world and between persons within each country. This changes our approach to poverty and forces us to examine personal and social responsibilities in a new light. In this way it gives us new perspectives for knowing how to discover—continuously—the face of the Lord in those of other persons, in particular those of the poor and the mistreated. And it allows us to go directly to what, theologically speaking, is decisive: positioning ourselves in the heart of the proclamation of the reign of God, the expression of the gratuitous love of the God of Jesus Christ

The vision evident in the formula "preferential option for the poor" is the most substantial part of the contribution to the universal church made by the life of the Latin American church and by liberation theology. The question posed at the beginning of these pages about the future of liberation theology must take into account its factual and contemporary connection to everything that option signifies. This perspective is obviously not something that belongs to liberation theology alone; the Christian message itself requires, and reveals the meaning of, a response to the poor in which God's gift of the reign is accepted. It is always a matter of a discourse on faith, which simply allows us to recall and reread in today's context (with all of the newness that context reveals to us) something that, in one way or another, has always been present— ceaselessly but not without interruptions—throughout the march of the people of God in history. It is good to stress this, not in order to diminish the contribution of liberation theology, whose destiny is tied to the biblical meaning of solidarity with the poor. Rather, we must outline correctly the degree to which this theology both stands in continuity and parts ways with previous theologies—and above all, with earlier Christian experiences and routes taken to witness to God's reign.

As in the two cases treated above, I am concerned here with making it clear that the very challenge arising from poverty also opens up perspectives that allow us to go on bringing forth "the new and the old"—from the treasure of the Christian message. Faith discernment must be lucid in this regard. But to assure this, we must overcome the obstinacy of seeing the world's poverty today as only a social problem. This would amount to disregarding what this painful sign of the times might have to say to us. All of this is summed up in the conviction that we must look at history from its underside, that is, from the side of its victims. The cross of Christ illuminates this vision and makes us understand it as a step toward the definitive victory of life in the Risen One.

Current Tasks

Let me indicate some areas in which certain tasks await the kind of theological reflection that concerns me. Naturally there would be many more things to say and clarifications to make, but this cannot be done in these few pages. I hope to treat them in greater detail in a single, longer work which is already begun.[8]

The Complexity of the World of the Poor

From the beginning, liberation theology took into account the different dimensions of poverty. To put it in other words—as in the

---

8. This will allow me to provide bibliographical references on these subjects which I am removing for now. Nevertheless, see those that are found in "¿Dónde dormirán los pobres?"

Bible—care was taken not to reduce poverty to its economic aspect, though of course this is important.[9] This led to the claim that the poor person is "insignificant," a person who is considered a "non-person," someone whose full rights as a human being are not recognized. We are talking about persons without social or individual weight, who count little in society or in the church. This is how they are seen or, more precisely, not seen, because they are in fact invisible insofar as they are excluded in today's world. The reasons for this are diverse: lacking material goods, of course, but also having a certain skin color, being a woman, belonging to a culture held in contempt (or considered important only because it is exotic, which, when all is said and done, amounts to the same thing). Poverty is, in fact, a complex and multifaceted reality. In speaking for decades about the rights of the poor (see, for example, the Medellín statement on peace), we were referring to the multidimensionality of poverty.

A second perspective, equally present from the very beginning, was seeing the poor as the others of a society constructed without regard for, or even over against, their most basic rights, far from their way of life and values. This is so true that when history is read from the vantage point of the outsider (a woman, for example), it becomes a different history.

---

9. This is expressed in formulas found in the first works of liberation theology. In reference to the poor, I spoke repeatedly of "peoples, races, and social classes" (*A Theology of Liberation: History, Politics, and Salvation,* trans. Caridad Inda and John Eagleson [rev. ed.; Maryknoll, NY: Orbis Books, 1988] 103; see also 116, 118) and of "exploited popular classes, oppressed cultures, and races discriminated against" (see my essay "Liberation Praxis and Christian Faith" [1973], published in *Power of the Poor in History* [Maryknoll, NY: Orbis Books, 1979] 37; see also 51, 60, 62, 64, and 70). Similar expressions are found in my essay "God's Revelation and Proclamation in History" (1976), in *Power of the Poor,* 18, 20-21, 22. Likewise, it was affirmed that "women from these sectors are doubly exploited, marginalized, and scorned" (found in my essay "Theology from the Underside of History" [1976], in *Power of the Poor,* 218 n. 54; and in my essay "The Historical Power of the Poor" [1976], in *Power of the Poor,* 102). See as well Gustavo Gutiérrez, "La mujer: La último de la ultimo," *Mujer y Sociedad* 44 (1991) 14-15.

Nevertheless, to reread history could seem to be a purely intellectual exercise if we failed to understand that this also involves remaking it. Within this framework of ideas, the conviction remains firm—despite all the limitations and obstacles of which I am well aware, especially today—that the poor themselves must take charge of their own destiny. In this regard, taking up again the trajectory of these concerns in the field of history, ever since a person and theologian like Las Casas first attempted to view things as if he were an Indian," remains a rich vein yet to be exploited. The first person to do so from firsthand experience was Guaman Poma. Only when we free ourselves from staring inertly, making prejudgments, and accepting certain categories uncritically will we be able to discover the other.

For this very reason, it is not enough to be aware of this complexity; we must deepen our awareness, enter into the details of the diversity, and notice its power to question us. But neither is it enough to notice the status of the poor person as other; this status must also be studied in greater detail and considered in its entire, challenging reality. This is the process in which we now find ourselves, thanks above all to the concrete commitments made in and from the world of poverty, stamped for the most part among us—as I have already noted—by some kind of experience of Christian faith. Theological reflection is nourished by this daily experience (which is already several decades old) and at the same time enriches it.

This concern has gone deeper in recent years. Valuable studies have made it possible to enter in a particularly fruitful way into several key aspects of this complexity. Indeed, along these lines today we find various efforts being made to conceptualize faith by beginning with the secular situation of marginalization and spoliation of the various indigenous peoples of our continent and of the black population, violently incorporated into our history centuries ago. In a variety of ways we have been witnesses during this period to the vigor and strength that the voice of these peoples has acquired, to the cultural and human richness they are ready to contribute, and to the facets of the Christian message that they allow us to see in all their starkness. To this we must add the dialogue with other religious conceptions that were able to survive the destruction of previous centuries. These are minority views today (though equally respectable because committed human beings hold them), but we must recognize, without trying to recreate them artificially, that they are present among us with their cultural and religious makeup.

The theological reflections that come from these universes are particularly demanding and new. The same is true of those that come from the inhuman, and therefore unacceptable, condition of women in our society, especially those who belong to the social and ethnic strata I have just recalled. In this area we are also witnessing rich and new theological perspectives carried forward above all by women, but which are important to and challenge everyone. One of the most fertile fields is that of reading the Bible from the perspective of the real situation of women. But of course there are many others that also enlarge our horizon for understanding the Christian faith. This is the time to note as well how much we can hope that a consideration of the feminine and masculine dimensions of the human being—and a dialogue between the two—will deepen our faith.

It may be opportune to note that this is not a matter of defending ancient cultures fixed in time or of proposing out-of-date projects that the historical process has gone beyond, as some tend to think. Culture is an endless creation, elaborated every day. We see this in very different ways in our cities. They are a crucible of races and cultures at their most popular; at the same time, however, they are cruel places, where distances between the different social sectors that inhabit them are increasing. Both things are experienced in the cities of a continent undergoing rapid urbanization. This universe-in-process, which to a great degree carries with it and transforms the values of traditional cultures, conditions the lived experience of faith and the proclamation of the reign of God; it is, therefore, a historical starting point for reflection of the theological kind.

Nevertheless, the tone that a faith-discourse legitimately takes on because it privileges the world of the poor should not make us lose sight of the larger picture of what is called into question by the situation of all the poor. Nor should we neglect the common terrain from which our languages and reflections start and on which they discourse: that of the insignificant, of their integral liberation, and of the Good News of Jesus directed preferentially to all of them. In fact, we must avoid at all costs letting necessary and urgent attention to the sufferings and hopes of the poor give rise to the useless search for private theological preserves. These would be the source of exclusivities and mistrust that, since in essence these are converging and complementary perspectives, end up weakening the daily fight of the dispossessed for life, justice, and respect for their cultural and religious values. The same goes for their fight for the right to be equal at the same time as being different.

The complexity of the universe of the poor and of the perspective of the other, as I have recalled, is today better delineated with all their problems and conflicts, but at the same time with all their promise. I will not try to locate all the theological currents that have arisen from this situation under a single rubric, for the diversity here is equally important. However, the obvious historical bonds among them, as well as the horizon of the complex world of the poor that they share and in which they are located, allow us to see them as fruitful expressions of the present tasks of theological reflection when carried out from the perspective of the dispossessed of our continent. They represent open quarries.

Globalization and Poverty

We are not with the poor if we are not against poverty, said Paul Ricoeur many years ago—that is, if we do not reject the condition that overwhelms such a huge part of humanity. It is not a matter of a merely emotional rejection; we must come to know what it is that causes poverty on the social, economic, and cultural levels. This requires the analytical tools that are provided by the human sciences, but like all scientific thought they work with hypotheses that allow us to understand the reality they seek to explain. This is the same as saying that they are called upon to change in the face of new phenomena. This is what is happening today in the face of the dominance of neoliberalism, which has been carried to power on the shoulders of an economy more and more independent of politics (and even more of ethics). This autonomy is due to something we have come to know by the somewhat barbarous term *globalization*.

As is well known, the reality designated by this term comes from the world of the media but has strong repercussions in the economic and social arena and in other fields of human activity. Nevertheless, the word is deceptive—because it makes us think that we stand before a single world, when in fact, and at this point in time, it leads ineluctably to its opposite: the exclusion of a part of humanity from the economic loop and from the so-called benefits of contemporary civilization. What we have is a more and more pronounced asymmetry. Millions of people are converted in this way into useless objects or into disposable objects that are thrown away after use. We are talking about those who remain outside the sphere of knowledge, the decisive element in the economy of our time and the most important axis of capital accumulation. It is worth noting that this polarization is the result of the way globalization is being carried out today. Globalization itself constitutes a fact that does not necessarily have to take its present course toward growing inequality, and, as we know, without equality there is no justice. We know this, but in our time the problem is becoming more urgent.[10]

Economic neoliberalism postulates a market without restrictions, expected to regulate itself by its own means, and subjects all social solidarity in this field to a harsh critique, accusing it not only of being ineffective in ending poverty but even of being one of the causes of poverty. That there have been cases of abuse in this regard is clear and widely recognized, but here we have a rejection in principle that leaves society's most fragile members out in the cold. One

---

10. See in this regard the penetrating studies of Norberto Bobbie, *Destra e sinistra: Ragioni e significati di una distinzione politica* (Rome: Donzelli, 1994).

of the consequences of this kind of thinking—and among the most painful and severe—is the foreign debt, which has left poor nations shackled and beaten down. This is a debt that grew spectacularly thanks to, among other things, the interest rates set by the very creditors themselves. Cancellation of this debt was one of the most concrete and important points of the convocation called by John Paul II to celebrate a Jubilee Year, in the biblical sense of the term, in the year 2000.

This dehumanization of the economy, begun quite a while ago, which tends to convert everything, including persons, into merchandise, has been condemned by a theology that exposes the idolatrous nature (in the biblical sense of the term) of this development. However, the situation today not only makes it increasingly urgent to point this out, but also provides new elements that allow us to make a deeper theological analysis. On the other hand, we are currently witnessing a strange effort to justify economic neoliberalism theologically by comparing, for example, multinational corporations with the Servant of Yahweh, attacked and vilified by all, but from which justice and salvation will nevertheless come. And this is to say nothing of the so-called theology of prosperity, which has very close links, of course, with the position I just mentioned. This has sometimes led people to postulate a certain parallelism between Christianity and neoliberal doctrines. Without denying these impressions, we might wonder how far such an effort can go when it reminds us of the attempt—at the opposite extreme—to refute Marxism by taking it as a kind of religion that supposedly paralleled, element for element, the Christian message (original sin and private property, the need for a redeemer and the proletariat, etc.). But of course this remark does not eliminate the need for a radical critique of the ideas prevailing today in the field of economics. Quite the contrary.

We cannot avoid doing theology by beginning with the poor, the favorites of God. This theology must take into account the autonomy proper to the discipline of economics and at the same time remain aware of its relation to the totality of the life of human beings. This requires, first of all, that we take up an ethical demand. For the same reason, while staying clear of the interplay among the positions I mentioned in the previous paragraph, we should not lose sight of the fact that the strongest rejection of neoliberal positions begins with the contradictions of an economy that cynically, and in the long run suicidally, forgets about the human being. In particular it forgets those who are defenseless in this field; today that means the majority of humankind. At issue is an ethical question, in the broadest sense of the term, that obliges us to look into the perverse mechanisms that distort from within that human activity that we call the economy. Valuable efforts at theological reflection along these lines are being made among us.

Within this problematic of globalization and poverty, we also need to situate the perspectives opened up by ecological concerns raised in the face of the destruction—equally suicidal—of the environment. These concerns have made us more sensitive to all the dimensions of the gift of life and have helped us to widen the horizon of social solidarity, which must include a respectful link to nature. This matter does not affect only the developed countries whose industries cause so much damage to the natural habitat of humanity; it affects everyone, including the poorest countries. It is not possible today to think theologically about poverty without taking into consideration these realities.

Deepening Spirituality

If the previous points were in one way or another already developed or intimated from the very beginning in liberation theology (which is not to deny, of course, what is new and creative in the work we have seen since then), the theme of spirituality was always a major concern. Not only is spirituality a matter of consequence to every Christian; the very fate of the kind of theology I have been proposing depends on it. Indeed, I have been deeply convinced for a long time—and am immensely indebted to the work of M. D. Chenu in this—that behind every faith-understanding is a way of following Jesus.[11] "Spirituality" is the word we use today to designate what is known in the gospels as "following Jesus." This is what forms the backbone of faith discourse. This is what gives theology its deepest meaning and its breadth. This is one of the main points in construing theology as a reflection on practice, the very heart of discipleship. Its two great and interconnected dimensions—prayer and commitment in history—make up what the Gospel of Matthew calls "doing the Father's will" in contrast to simply saying "Lord, Lord" (7:21). Thus, the claim that "our methodology is our spirituality" takes on meaning.[12] Both are paths to God, and we have to keep moving forward along them.

In recent years we have seen an abundance of publications along the lines of a liberation spirituality. The reason is simple: in the midst of a historical process that has known both successes and failures, the spiritual experience of the poor in Latin America has matured. Interest in spirituality in no way signifies a withdrawal from social commitments that for us remain totally in effect as expressions of solidarity with the poor and oppressed. Those who think otherwise seem innocent of the radicalness that comes from getting to the deepest level of things where love for God and love for the neighbor are united every day. Spirituality is located at this depth. Far from being an evasion of the challenges of the present, it provides steadfastness and durability to the commitments to which I just alluded. Rilke was right when he said that God is found in our roots. And we never finish deepening them.

In the very nucleus of the preferential option for the poor is a spiritual element: the experience of God's gratuitous love. The rejection of injustice and of the oppression it implies is anchored in our faith in the God of life. It is not surprising, therefore, that

---

11. See his famous *Une école de théologie: Le Saulchoir* (Paris: Cerf, 1985; originally published in 1937).

12. Gustavo Gutiérrez, "The Historical Power of the Poor" (1978), in *Power of the Poor in History*, 103-4.

this option has been signed and sealed with the blood of those who, as Archbishop Romero used to say, have died with the "mark of a martyr." Besides the case of the archbishop of San Salvador himself, this is the reality suffered by numerous Christians on a continent that at the same time claims to be Christian. We cannot leave aside this cruel paradox in considering the spirituality of Latin America. The truth is that in many ways the experience of the cross marks the daily life of Latin American and Peruvian Christians.[13]

What is fundamental within this framework of ideas is the spiritual journey of people who live out their faith and maintain their hope in the midst of a daily lot of poverty and marginalization but also of plans and a greater awareness of their rights. The poor of Latin America have embarked upon the road of affirming their human dignity and their status as daughters and sons of God. On this journey there is an encounter with the Lord, crucified and risen. To be attentive to this spiritual experience and to gather up the oral accounts and writings that narrate it become an indispensable task of theological reflection done by Latin Americans. "Drinking from their own well": that is what I once called this moment, using an expression from Bernard of Clairvaux. Their own waters show us the degree to which Christian faith has been inculturated in those peoples who are poor but also possess a culture and a historical trajectory different from those we find in the North Atlantic world.

What I have just said follows from what was noted above, namely, that Latin Americans are, for the most part, both poor and believing. At the heart of a situation that excludes and mistreats them and from which they seek to liberate themselves, the poor believe in the God of life. As our friends Victor (now deceased) and Irene Chero said to John Paul II in the name of the poor of Peru—more than a million of whom were present for the occasion—during the pope's 1985 visit to our country, "With our hearts broken by suffering, we see our wives pregnant while ill with tuberculosis, our babies dying, our children growing up weak and without a future." And they added, "But despite all of this, we believe in the God of life."

---

13. See the excellent works of Jon Sobrino on these themes.

This is a context, or rather a living reality, that reflection on faith cannot avoid. On the contrary, such reflection must be nourished by it—unceasingly.

Let me say a few words by way of conclusion. If, as might be expected, I have emphasized the challenge that comes from the world of poverty, I in no way think that the other two questions do not affect us in Latin America and the Caribbean. Theological reflection in the Christian world must face all three of the afore-mentioned challenges and also clarify their interrelationships. I have barely touched on them in these pages, but I am convinced of the importance and fruitfulness of establishing their interconnection.

To do this we will have to avoid the temptation of pigeonholing by assigning these challenges to the different continents: the challenge of modernity to the Western world, that of poverty to Latin America and Africa, and that of religious pluralism to Asia. This would be a simplistic solution that overlooks the interactions and points of contact among different peoples and cultures today. It also ignores the speed of communications, which we are now witnessing and which gives rise to a sense of closeness felt by people who are geographically far apart.

Naturally there are emphases proper to the diverse regions of humanity. But they are only that—accents. At the present we are called to a theological task that takes new routes and maintains with a firm hand both the particularity and the universality of the reality we are experiencing. This mission cannot be carried out apart from a great sensitivity to the diverse challenges I have recalled or without a respectful and open dialogue that takes as its historical starting point all aspects of the conditions in which human beings are living, as well as the condition of their dignity. This holds in a special way for the poor and the excluded, who, for Christians, reveal the presence of the God of Jesus Christ among us.

We stand before a stimulating and promising mission in which there remains much for liberation theology to do and, above all, to learn.

—Translated by James B. Nickoloff

CHAPTER 4

Liberation Theology in Context

GERHARD LUDWIG MÜLLER

The Necessity for a Theology of Liberation

In recent years, public interest in Latin-American liberation theology has apparently ebbed away. Conflicts about church teachings have shifted from the theological realm to the sphere of ecclesiastical discipline and church politics.

Should the theology of liberation again receive widespread attention? Should it even become a fashionable movement similar to a psychological movement that bursts into the public consciousness?

Everyone would like to value this singular phenomenon that unites a wide range of commitments. It is uncontestable that society in Latin America—indeed, in the entire Third World—remains a catastrophe. It was out of this reality that liberation theology originated as a theological achievement that is not only a clarification and a strategy for change but also a theological response that brought into view the concrete social, economic, and historical conditions of human existence as seen from the most noble standpoint of the human spirit and in the light of God's Word.

A theological exposé of concrete human conditions must continue to be the task of an inquiring, advancing theology within the universal church. Certainly, liberation theology has its origins in the social-economic contexts of the Third World. In this, it shows its originality: its ties to its contextual frame of reference. Since it is always connected to a specific context, it cannot generate a world-wide, unifying theology, for as such it would need to rely on unfortunate abstraction; that is, it would then become a theology removed from its actual relationships, a theology that formulates the truth of the gospel within a self-enclosed logic of pure concepts. Theology as an intellectual activity must be abstract, in the right sense of the word. Yet, it must also make known the concrete essence of what is manifest within the entire phenomenological realm of a specific, comprehended reality. Thus every theology must be contextually determined.

That said, theology itself must not splinter into an innumerable set of regional theologies. We may ask whether we "can cut a slice" from other theologies, which in themselves have nothing to do with us. Every regional theology must be oriented within itself toward the universal church. This universal-church dimension of every regional theology is grounded in theology's common object in that no society with its culture is totally isolated, existing for itself. Rather, it stands even in its socio-cultural context in interdependence with the entire development of humanity. Moreover, the universal-church dimension of a theology also comes about because of the inquirer, the knowing subject, who engages in this theology. Theologians must think in relation to universal history and universal society as they reflect on the coherence of God's Word to one humanity and one history.

The objective and subjective unity of universal theology originates not by means of an absolutizing of a regional theology (for example, in a Eurocentrism). Rather, this universality realizes itself because of a communications network of regional theologies. Concretely speaking, I am engaged in Latin American liberation theology because an objective dimension of my own existence consists of the societal, economic, and ecclesial relationships of people in Latin America, with their encompassing historical and religious conditions, and also because my theological understanding of God's revelation is only possible in relation to the universal, eschatological realization of salvation in the history of the human family.

There is no hidden motive at work here. There is no attempt to be engaged in daily conversations with liberation theologians in order to make liberation theology into a steady contributor to theological discussions. Rather, every theology must be directed in itself by the subject matter and the method, which in effect make the concern of liberation theology an aspect of all theologies that are attentive to their socio-economic frameworks.

We who are European theologians interact with liberation theology not simply because it exists or simply because it is interesting to engage ourselves in other themes. Rather, we engage ourselves in liberation theology because it represents a necessary regional theology, without which the entire process of communication in theology cannot function.

It was in this sense that Pope John Paul II clarified in a letter to the Brazilian conference of bishops in 1986 "that the theology of liberation is not only opportune but also valuable and necessary."[1] We must appreciate liberation theology's immediate background in the new, official understanding of the church that was adopted by the Second Vatican Council, especially in its Dogmatic Constitution on the Church, *Lumen gentium*, and in its Pastoral Constitution on the Church in the Modern World, *Gaudium et spes*. Further, the effort for a concrete transference of the council's stimulus to the Latin American church found its expression in the documents and the broad official consensus of the Second and Third Conferences of the Latin American bishops at Medellín (1968) and Puebla (1979). Moreover, the Congregation for the Doctrine of the Faith's "instructions" concerning liberation theology in 1984 and 1986—which differed from each other and yet were valuable—do not call into question the possibility of an authentic and original liberation theology but acknowledge its necessity.

If we intend to interact with liberation theology in its particulars, then we cannot study it from the position of "privileged officials" who are scrutinizing this theology for its positive and negative aspects, for its merits and drawbacks, as though assembling

---

1. Pope John Paul II, *Herder Korrespondenz* 40 (1986) 260.

an annual business report. To engage ourselves intellectually and spiritually with liberation theology requires that we enter into its theological reasoning and, in participation with the societal and ecclesial process of the church in Latin America, seek to determine liberation theology's specific ecclesial and theological place in the historical process of the world church. Within this participation, it is possible to highlight the critically differentiating and thus constructive contributions of liberation theology to the entire ecclesial communication of theology.

The Original Theological Approach of Liberation Theology

The concepts of liberation theology have a specific meaning for each of their most significant representatives. For this reason, some commentators have said that there is no one liberation theology but rather a loose set of liberation theologies. However, as careful study shows, there is no incoherent pluralism here. The broad spectrum of nuances is held together by a common theme, a unifying basic orientation, and an identical epistemological-theoretical starting point in method. Authoritative still is the first great systematization in the book *A Theology of Liberation* by Gustavo Gutiérrez, who with full right also bears the name "father of liberation theology." Since 1971, when this book first appeared, it has clearly generated an extensive and intensive broad development in theology. At once, the entire thematic of Catholic dogmatic and moral theology is successively laid out from this methodical starting point. Yet since 1971 the starting point has been clearly explained epistemologically and methodologically in response to the numerous objections and questions. This explanation was provided by Clodovis Boff in his book *Theology and Praxis: Epistemological Foundations* (1978).[2]

---

2. Clodovis Boff, *Theology and Praxis: Epistemological Foundations*, trans. Robert R. Barr (Maryknoll, NY: Orbis Books, 1987; reprint, Eugene, OR: Wipf & Stock, 2009).

From what does liberation theology's stimulus arise? It is a widespread misunderstanding to place the starting point solely in the catastrophic social and economic situation (as seen from every perspective) of the majority of people in the Third World. It is not simply that some Christians have asked what they as believers and theologians can do against the hunger, exploitation, injustice, wretched medical care, childhood mortality, premature death, the failure of every possible form of higher education, in short, against the inhuman living conditions that ruin human beings in body and soul. If this condition were liberation theology's sole starting point, someone could simply be content with the church's classical social teachings. However, along with its social involvement, the theology of liberation's starting point at an epistemological level includes the social sciences and national economics. With this point of departure, it could happen that liberation theology would be reduced at best to a form of intellectual inquiry that is auxiliary to the social sciences. But this reduction has not happened.

Liberation theology in itself wants to be pure theology in its method and results. For the definition of theology, one can appropriately recall that of Thomas Aquinas: "God is the object of this science. . . . But in this sacred science, all things are treated under the aspect of God: either because they are God himself or because they refer to God as their beginning and end."[3] Liberation theology is driven by the strict use of the word theology. In this orientation, it undertakes a description of the real world and the things of the world insofar as they relate to God. It holds that a description and comprehension of the actual relationships in which people interact are not possible without the assistance of the empirical sciences, in other words, of the social sciences, political science, and economics. It draws on sociology and the other sciences as forms of intellectual inquiry that are auxiliary to theology.

The theology of liberation does not ask, What should a Christian say about the Third World's injustices that scream out to heaven?

---

3. Thomas Aquinas, *Summa theologiae*, I, q. 1, a. 7.

Rather, it poses the theologically fashioned question, How can someone speak about God, Christ, the Holy Spirit, the church, the sacraments, grace, and eternal life in light of the misery, exploitation, and oppression of people in the Third World, especially when we conceive of human beings as the reality created in God's image (Genesis 1:26-27), the reality for whom Christ died so that in all realms of life human beings would experience God as salvation and life itself (Romans 8:18-39)?

In response to this question, liberation theologians clearly proceed from a biblical understanding of God. According to the Bible, God is not the abstract Absolute, the Beyond or the Other, separate from our material world, existing outside of historical time and encountering us in the other-worldly interiority of a purely spiritual soul. Instead, God has created the world and human beings in a spiritual-material unity. In creation, history, and their ultimate completion, God makes the reality of life available to the world and human beings. God is the God of life and salvation, the God who offers and realizes salvation and life for human beings in their spiritual-bodily unity of personal existence within the unified creaturely, social, and historical world.

Salvation occurs therefore not in an otherworldly, beyond-time, transcendent, alternative other world that hovers as a second floor over the ground floor of the secular, profane, and historical world. In this dualist view, the profane, earthly world is a vale of tears for the majority of people, and it is a paradise for a minority. In this perspective, our earthly world at best has to do with salvation in an "other world." And, our immortal souls secure the expectation of good fortune in this "other world" by means of devotional exercises and morally proper relationships. Sins happen from our neglect of religious practices such as prayer and liturgy and also from our immoral conduct in the violation of individual commandments, which God established for us as purely formal tests of our obedience. Sins are not regarded as offenses against God and God's intention for the salvation and life of every human being.

This dualistic view of well-being in this world and of salvation in the "other world"—a salvation that is promised today and fulfilled in the future [beyond this life]—is the basis of Marxism's powerful accusation that the Christian religion is an ideology of consolation that functions to preserve society's injustice and exploitation. When we become aware of the dualism between worldly well-being and other-worldly salvation, we cannot simply dismiss the partial truth of the Marxist view. Moreover, someone still remains within the presuppositions of the dualistic starting point when one naively offers here the solution of *et . . . et . . .* , that is, of salvation *both* in this life *and also* in the next life. It is also inadequate when someone reacts in thoughtless defiance to the Marxist critique by countering with the argument that suffering in this life can be a way to salvation in the next. This argument includes praise for "the poor in spirit" who are "blessed" and promised "the kingdom of heaven" [Matthew 5:3].

At this point, the limits of the classic Catholic social teachings become evident. Before noting them, however, let's not deny the merits of these teachings. These merits include the social teachings' emphasis on the priority of work over capital, on social affiliations [e.g., labor unions], on private property as a means of production and as production's basis and ground, on the access of all human beings to the material goods of the earth, and, in extraordinary cases, on the right of people to defensive opposition to extreme political systems of exploitation and the violation of human rights.

But the church's social teachings are limited because they are cast in a certain sense still in a dualistic framework. They assume that, on the one side, there stands the natural world whose laws and orders are accessible to human reason operating independently of its historical situation, and that, on the other side, there is the supernatural order of grace. Correspondingly, the state is responsible for the *temporalia*, the temporal realm, in which the church only partially assists in the formulation of the principles and goals of justice as well as in the well-being of all people. These goals are supposedly accessible to natural reason, even without epistemological recourse to supernatural faith and the help of God's grace. The church is primarily responsible for the *spiritualia*, the spiritual realm.

In order to move out of the powerful attraction of these dualistic categories, which have governed Christian dogmatic theology beyond Platonism and idealism, one must operate in the thought form of the biblical-Hebraic unity of thought and life. One must begin from the experience of God as the originator both of the world's creation and redemption and also of each human being's personal wholeness in his or her spiritual–bodily existence, which is both individual and social. It is from this point forward that the entire thematic of theology must be formally reconceived.

On the basis of this shift, there now follows a new methodological understanding of theology. To put it somewhat schematically, *classical theology* could be described as the theoretical comprehension of reality and of God's constitutive work in the world. Yet, the more *existential-anthropological theology* of the last century has asked, What is the meaning of God, revelation, and grace for a human being, and what do they contribute to someone's self-understanding? Further, *liberation theology* understands that theological inquiry is related to people's active, transforming, and practical participation in God's initiated and comprehensive liberating action— the action through which God qualifies history to be one process of efficacious freedom. Someone's participation in God's transforming action liberates him or her, and thus it makes this person into an active collaborator in God's process of liberation.

The differentiation between theory and praxis, between theoretical theology and practical theology, is now impossible. Theology does not comprehend reality first theoretically and conceptually and then afterward attempt to apply the ideas of faith to concrete material reality. It also does not advance as though it arises out of a thoughtless activism that magically and mythically generates the truth of ideas out of itself. Praxis—along with the primacy of praxis—involves a person's holistic encounter with reality and his or her participation in the process of reality's social and historical realization. As someone participates intelligently and creatively in the process of reality, that individual's intellect is defined by reality as the principle of comprehension, and this intellect then comes to a fullness of comprehension.

This movement that begins with praxis is, however, nothing other than the classically grasped relationship of faith and love. In faith, someone fully orients himself or herself to God's self-communicating love. In doing this, a human being becomes united in love with God, who is the energy and power of personal faith (Galatians 5:6). As a result, this individual participates in a collaborative manner in God's active and liberating love of all human beings. Only the faith that is active in love and whose inner form and reality are love entirely experiences the gift of grace or, in a comprehensive social and eschatological connection, the gift of God's kingdom. In this regard, Gutiérrez writes:

> Love is the nourishment and the fullness of faith, the gift of one's self to the Other, and invariably to others. This is the foundation of the *praxis* of Christians, of their active presence in history. According to the Bible, faith is the total human response to God, who saves through love. In this light, the understanding of faith appears as the understanding not of the simple affirmation—almost memorization—of truths, but of a commitment, an overall attitude, a particular posture toward life.[4]

Therefore, theology does not undertake an abstract and theoretical relationship to reality. Instead, theologians first participate with their minds and their actions in the transforming process of history, which is a history of liberation by God. In a second step of reflection, they come to a spiritual-intellectual [that is, theological] grasp of this process. In a third step, their participation in the process of liberation and critical reflection upon it lead to an intellectually understood transformation of reality directed toward its God-given goal.

To repeat, the realization of theology occurs by means of a threefold method. First, Christians participate through action, suffering, and comprehension in God's praxis of the liberation of

---

4. Gutiérrez, *A Theology of Liberation* (2014) 6.

human beings in history. Second, through the light of the gospel, they engage in a critical and rational reflection on this praxis. (This critical reflection is theology in the strict sense.) Third and finally, Christians undertake a critically understood transformation of reality. In all of this, they have in view the liberating of the freedom of each human being in God's ultimate kingdom.

Throughout this process, there results an option for the people who need to be freed and who participate actively and consciously in the faith that is set free in the process of liberation. These people are those who are oppressed, poor, and suffering. God's liberating action empowers them to become personal subjects. As such, they not only receive passively the gift of freedom, but at the same time they become collaborators in God's liberation process. They move from being objects for assistance from the state and the church to being personal subjects who actively undertake and cooperate with God's process of liberation.

Given this personal development, the church is no longer the church *for* the people but the church *of* the people. The people of God become personal subjects who in their actions drive history forward toward the goal of fully realized freedom. As in the teachings of Vatican II, the church is not only an institution that administers salvation. The church as a whole—with its inner organization of laity and hierarchy—becomes a sign of and an instrument for God's community with human beings and for human beings' community with one another. The church is actively the sacrament of God's kingdom or the salvation of the world.

This understanding is also the original sense of the "base communities." "Base" is not used here in opposition to the hierarchy. It means that the community as a whole—with its inner composition and the emergence of differing charisms, services, and offices— becomes the personal subject of liberating actions and the historical praxis of liberation. Thus, there results also the historical empowering of poor people insofar as they participate as personal subjects in the historical process and in its realization as they become personal subjects of the action of liberation.

The newness of liberation theology exists not in that it introduces into theology new themes or that it aims for a different content in divine revelation. Its essential newness exists in a new starting point and in a new method by means of which the classical content of Catholic theology is newly and thoroughly conceived. Commenting on liberation theology's originality, Gutiérrez writes:

> It is for all of these reasons that the theology of liberation offers us not so much a new theme for reflection as a *new way* to do theology. Theology as critical reflection on historical praxis is a liberating theology, a theology of the liberating transformation of the history of humankind and also therefore that part of humankind—gathered into *ecclesia*—which openly confesses Christ. This is a theology which does not stop with reflecting on the world. But rather tries to be part of the process through which the world is transformed. It is a theology which is open—in the protest against trampled human dignity, in the struggle against the plunder of the vast majority of humankind, in liberating love, and in the building of a new, just, and comradely society—to the gift of the Kingdom of God.[5]

Theology as critical reflection (occurring as the second step, above) unfolds in three modes of mediation or reflection (which are explained in the next section). These three modes are:

1. social-analytic reflection
2. a hermeneutical, systematic reflection
3. a practical-pastoral reflection and application.

Thus, unlike many critics, one must notice that the social-analytic reflection is not placed ahead of theology in such a way that this initial mediation consists merely of profane scientific-sociological theory. Rather, this first step is already part of theology itself insofar as theology (drawing on the social sciences) sees the concrete social situation at the outset in light of the experiences of God as the

---

5. Gutiérrez, *A Theology of Liberation* (2014) 12.

creator and liberator of every human being. While this first theological step is undertaken with the help of social-scientific analysis, it remains a strictly theological endeavor.

Liberation Theology in Its Realization

The Social-Analytic Reflection

Liberation theology assumes that our relationship with God and our situation in the world and society belong together. Since a human being is a spiritual-material unity who is mediated in oneself, an individual's relationship with God cannot be separated from the societal and social conditions in which his or her human life is historically realized. Conversely, a disturbance in someone's relationship with God shows itself in antagonistic social relationships. It is uncontestable that societal structures, especially in South America, insofar as they degrade the majority of people to the level of nonhuman beings, evince and result from the loss of God, and thus they are an obstacle to experiencing God as the God of life.

The conditions of oppression, injustice, and misery that exist in Latin America bear no resemblance to social romanticism's depiction of a simple and unassuming life. Poverty here means simply nothing other than death. What are the origins of this extensive and fatal poverty? Poverty here is not simply the consequence of individual misfortune or of a personal inability to master life. Rather, it is a structural and inevitable condition of human existence that destroys the lives of most human beings.

In order to attain an initial comprehension of this reality, one is able to employ the empirical sciences with their social-science tools. In this empirical study, there is also a reliance on a Marxist analysis of contemporary society under industrial- and capitalist-oriented economic conditions. There is no doubt that liberation theology wants nothing to do with the ideological totalitarianism of communism with a Leninist and Stalinist stamp. One makes one's own the (Marxist) insight that a human life does not exist apart from its historical and societal conditions, and that even a grasp of the truth of these conditions cannot be had without a consideration of the influence of self-interest on an observer's point of view. Certainly, there exists a materialistic starting point in communism. This starting point stands at odds with idealism but not necessarily at odds with Christian belief, which itself is rooted in an anthropology that arises out of the spiritual-corporeal unity of a human being and which simultaneously keeps in view both the spiritual reality of human life and also its realization in the world's material conditions of existence.

In contrast to Marxism, liberation theology conceives of a human being not simply as a product and as a composite of his or her material conditions. Instead, a human being is the person created and called by God, the person who is the personal subject and bearer of reality and thus also the shaper of the material conditions of human existence in the economic and social realm. As God liberates a human being and desires to make him or her into a personal subject, the actual realization of personal subjectivity and freedom occurs only as the conditions under which the individual's free subjectivity is to be realized are themselves transformed. Therefore, a human being becomes a personal subject in the process of the transformation of history. And, as a human being participates in the transforming process of history, he or she simultaneously creates the prerequisites for participating in the process of understanding humanity in the light of the gospel.

The opposite of liberation is oppression. Oppression originates out of dependence (subordination). Dependence means that life's material conditions are so limited that the free subjectivity of a human being cannot develop. The structures of dependence do not come about because of destiny and natural conditions. To claim otherwise would be to espouse a false fatalism, according to which there purportedly exists a divinely intended division within humanity between the oppressors and the oppressed, the rich and the poor, the masters and the slaves. Instead, the global dependence that encompasses the world is the result of a historical process and its contemporary continuation.

During the colonization of South America, the distinct cultural and economic relationships already existing among the continent's indigenous cultures disappeared. (At this point, we have no intention of giving a retrospective, romanticized explanation of what happened, for although there was little material poverty in the cultures of the Incas and the Aztecs, the freedom of a person was not at its best. An unreflective state-absolutism governed the situation.) With colonization, Latin America became a provider of raw materials and the back country of the economic centers in Europe and North America. There occurred a reciprocal interaction. The prosperity at the center relied on the pushing of Latin America to the periphery. There were the economic systems of mercantilism and then of the modern industrial capitalism of the central nations and their agents in the all-powerful multinational corporations, which produced the Third World's marginalization and an impoverishment of its broad mass of people.

It changes nothing in the ultimate outcome when individual representatives of industrial, capitalist corporations are people of good will. Within the world's economic system, there are at work the objective, powerful laws that generate the interdependence of the center and the periphery of the economic system in the world. While capitalism in European institutions is now socially and civilly domesticated, the fact nevertheless remains that the nations and the international capitalist institutions in the world arena interrelate in a purely capitalist mode according to the principle of an unconditional maximization of profits at the expense of the people who are weak.

To call attention to this capitalism one need only mention some key, familiar concepts: the cheap wages in the "other" countries; the availability of cheap, raw materials; the orientation of agricultural production not to the needs of the indigenous people but for luxury products in the First World; the flight of capital to the people making a profit; the international allocation of credit for the establishing of an infrastructure for an industrialization in which there exists tax-abatement for outside investors. The result is that the nations at the periphery as a rule must pay back loans with high interest and compounded interest without being free to share in the indigenous industrial complexes by means of taxation, since their profits flow back to the mother institutions in the nations at the center of the economic system.

The current economic system is problematic in other ways as well. To be named are the compulsory measures of the World Bank and of the international currency funds that require nations to seek credit which is possible only by the raising of taxes within their countries and by the cancellation of their governments' subvention for basic foodstuffs, which abruptly has the immediate consequence of greater misery with greater hunger among the poorest of the poor people. Also to be named are the indigenous powerful elites and the dissipation of a nation's domestic finances in unproductive military defenses and in senseless objects of prestige.

The unequal influence between the periphery and the center is systemic. (Of course, this systemic inequality does not exclude ecclesial and private measures of help that express good will and also represent often necessary immediate assistance. But these efforts cannot bring about a fundamental change in the economic system.) Further, it does not suffice in this economic structure to appeal to the good will of the ruling people and the owners. Because the relationships between the people with wealth and the people in poverty are structurally determined, one must go to the roots of the misery and initiate a global process of liberation from the current economic system.

Liberation theology uses the term capitalism to name the financial structure that produces oppression and exploitation in Latin America. What is meant here is not simply an economic system in which free enterprise has an important place. In this context, capitalism means the combination of money and material means of power in the hands of an oligarchy and the international centers of business and power. As an alternative, liberation theology speaks of socialism. With this proposal, there is clearly intended not a planned and ordered economy. What is intended here is an economic system with the goal of the active participation of all people in the economies of their respective countries and also of the active participation of the underdeveloped nations in the global economic process.

Insofar as the powerful elites have controlled the preservation of the wealth and its surplus amid the exploitation and the oppression of the broad mass of people, liberation theology speaks in this regard of a class conflict from above. It views society as an arena for the conflict of interests. It sees that by and large history has unfolded not out of a harmonious development of the potentialities among people but out of the antagonism of opposing principles and interests. In this perspective, the opposition at present between the First World and the Third World is clearly a historical manifestation of the general antagonism operating throughout history.

Liberation theology perceives that at its depths there is reflected in this antagonism on the level of the societal and historical situation the ultimate opposition in human affairs between grace and sin. While the theology of liberation partially adopts the language of Marxism when it talks about class conflict, it aims not at a negation of the people of one economic class by the people of a lower economic class. It does not intend an awkward change in places between the people who oppress and the people who are oppressed, between those who exploit and those who are exploited.

In the Christian perspective, all people participate in the conflict of grace against sin. More specifically, all people share in the incarnation of salvation in a society's life-shaping social structures and in the overcoming of sin and sin's objectification in exploitative economic systems. Grace and sin do not exist idealistically and spiritually pure in themselves but always in connection with their embodiment and materialization in actual human relationships. In this sense, liberation theology holds that grace and sin have differing political dimensions. One could perhaps speak more accurately of the social dimension insofar as one must politically limit the concept of grace and sin to modern nontotalitarian nations with regard to the management of free social energies and their interactions.

This insight into the societal character of grace and sin is surely not as new as it may seem. In the classical doctrine of grace one always speaks of an ecclesial and thus also a social dimension of grace and its embodiment in good works, that is, even in contemporary forms. In the classical doctrine of original sin it is already said that sin initially arose out of the misuse of free will, which then corrupted the nature of human beings, that is, the whole network of our material and spiritual conditions of life. Seen in light of our depraved nature, it is clear that the self-transcendence of the person in relation to God and neighbors in faith and love is now impossible (on our own).[6] Thus, it is understood also that the redeemed and liberated human nature can be realized anew only in relation to the person of the new human being, the new Adam, in other words, in relation to Christ. Because our nature is now liberated from the conditions of the nature estranged from God, we as new human beings, who are created by God in salvation and justification, and we also as persons liberated for freedom are able to act in a new manner so that we participate in God's liberating action in history.

The Hermeneutical, Systematic-Theological Reflection

In this second step, liberation theology now interprets the experience of exploitation and the analysis of its historical and social conditions in the light of divine revelation. The biblical testimony shows us God as the creator who chooses history as the place of God's liberating action. God's act of redemption has liberated human beings not from history but for history as the arena for the realization of material conditions appropriate for human beings in their actualization into spiritual persons. The message concerning God's creation is interpreted in full connection with God's historical action of redemption. This message shows us the origin and goal of human beings who are created in God's image, who as personal realities always actualize ourselves in matter, that is, in worldly and

---

6. On the doctrine of grace and original sin, see Thomas Aquinas, *Summa theologiae*, III, q. 69, a. 3; I-II, q. 81, a. 1; q. 82, a. 1, ad. 2; III, q. 8, a. 5, ad 1.

bodily ways. God's historical actions in relation to creation, which has fallen from God into sin, always occur in the sign both of the salvation of human beings and also of the liberation from self-produced conditions of enslavement, conditions that obstruct human beings from community with God and their neighbors in love.

In the perspective of the Bible, this process of redemption shows itself fundamentally in the exodus experience. Salvation is situated not simply in the interiority of the soul that was not touched by the Egyptian whips. God promised the oppressed Israelites not simply a better, differently conceived heavenly life. Instead, salvation occurs in God's actual liberating action, in God's overcoming of the Israelites' slavery. This saving event is something completely other than an immanent or horizontal abridgement (of salvation). God's liberating action, which also encompasses life's material conditions, leads to God's covenant with Israel. This covenant is the inner aim of liberation. Liberation is the outer manifestation of the covenant, namely, of the personal and communal loving union of human beings with God.

In relation to the historical form of the realization of salvation there is actually also a transcendence of salvation. However, the transcendence of salvation exists not in a spatial-temporal realm beyond earthly life, in a world behind creation. There is only the one creation of God in relation to which a human being can stand in a different manner. The transcendence of salvation in relation to a human being's historical actualization happens not at the point of one's individual death or at the collective end of human history. Rather, there occurs the fullness of the transcendence of salvation insofar as God becomes the absolute content of our personal self-transcendence, for example, in the intuition of God and in the ever-lasting community of love.

At the same time, there occurs also the fullness of the immanence of salvation, namely, in that the encompassing historical-social and material interrelationships of our creaturely existence are newly defined by God, for example, in the resurrection of the body, the communion of the saints, and the creation of the new heaven and the new earth. God in God's very self is the absolute content of salvation both in the transcendental-personal relationship of a human being with God and also in the completion and restoration of the material conditions of life of embodied human beings existing in creation, although in a manner that is hidden from our current intuitive representation.

In Christian faith, salvation as presented in the New Testament is thoroughly misunderstood when someone tries to spiritualize it in contrast to what is purported to be the Old Testament's "this-worldly" and materialist view of salvation.

Liberation theology—through its interpretation of scripture, in particular, of the prophetic critique—puts into perspective superficial cultic or religious activity that loses sight of love of God and neighbor. It highlights God's special partiality for the people who are poor and marginalized; this partiality expresses itself in the prophetic literature, especially in the messianic promise of "Good News" for poor people, which is found in Second Isaiah (Isaiah 40–55).

The New Testament in general and the Synoptic Gospels in particular focus on the action of the kingdom of God. Jesus proclaims his "Good News" for people who are poor, imprisoned, oppressed, suffering in body or soul, and pushed to society's margins. He has come for sinners and not for the righteous. In this message, Jesus' option for people in poverty is established, especially insofar as the people who are poor embody or represent all human beings who seek God's salvation and liberation from the relationships that burden them. Jesus' healing/salvation of ill people shows the inner connection between salvation as God's eschatological arrival in the humanity of Jesus, God's new covenant, and salvation as the realization of the healing of human beings' corporeal conditions of life. The corporeal healing is simultaneously an anticipation of the eschatological immanence of salvation.

On the one hand, Jesus was completely other than a social reformer or a political agent. He did not want to cure the symptoms. He has brought comprehensively the kingdom of God, which also overcomes in principle the symptoms of sin in unjust social structures. On the other hand, Jesus was also not the proclaimer of an other-worldly mysticism or of a disembodied asceticism. Jesus' preaching and actions revealed the unity of salvation's transcendent and immanent aspects.

Jesus' death by crucifixion cannot be considered as an other-worldly religiosity that separates creation from redemption. Instead, Jesus died in order to demonstrate God's world-transforming and liberating love in relation to the opposition of sinners. The crucifixion of Jesus has drawn the world and history into the thorough-going new creation. Therefore, (at the Last Supper) Jesus spoke about the new covenant in his flesh and blood (1 Cor 11:25; Mark 14:25). Whoever seeks Christ outside the embodiment and worldliness of one's human existence does not find him. But whoever eats his flesh, that is, communicates with his incarnational reality, has eternal life and thus community with God and with the transcendence of salvation.

The cross of Jesus manifests itself as the revelation of God's option for those who are poor. God is engaged in the comprehensive process of history on the side of the people who are oppressed in order to lead them to freedom and to make it possible for them to participate in the realization of the salvation promised by God to all human beings. In this sense Gutiérrez speaks of the justice of the historical power of the people in poverty. When poor people participate in the process of salvation, they enter into history and move out of their marginal situation and loss of meaning. However, God also remains committed to the people who exploit others and rule over others; God seeks to liberate them from the anxiety that makes them seize life for themselves at the expense of other people's well-being. God makes it possible for those who exploit and those who rule to find true freedom. In Jesus' resurrection, God has shown what life actually is and how we can translate freedom into society's tangible structures through our being-there-for-others. God manifests God's self as the Father of all human beings, as their brother in Christ, and as their friend in the Holy Spirit. God makes it possible for them to live in freedom, solidarity, and equality.

3. *The Pastoral-Practical Reflection*

At this point, the social-analytic reflection (#1 above) and the systematic theological reflection (#2 above) converge in the action of Christ's church. The church can be God's church only when its goal is not simply to uphold its existence and influence as an organization and an institution. To paraphrase a statement by Dietrich Bonhoeffer, the church can be God's church only when it is the church for others. As such, it must participate in God's liberating action in history. In continuity with the teachings of the Second Vatican Council, this view means that the church is a sign of and instrument for the union of God with human beings and the communion of human beings with one another. The church exists in the service of God's goal for the human family in history.

Unacceptable is the alternative that "either God alone brings the kingdom of God at the end of time, or human beings realize the kingdom of God, which would therefore be only the kingdom of human making." Also to be excluded, on the basis of the theology of grace, is the effort to separate and to quantify the divine contribution and the human contribution to the coming of God's kingdom. God's grace and human freedom (and action) exist in a relationship different from this quantified view. In fact, God shares God's self with us as the content of human freedom, and God gives God's self as the goal of a human being's movement to freedom, as the goal to which human freedom dynamically moves for its historical and material completion. This orientation manifests the transcendence of salvation.

At the same time, God brings about transcendental and categorical salvation in history so that a human being is not disconnected from human affairs but becomes increasingly engaged as a bearer of history and a shaper of the world and society. This orientation evinces the immanence of salvation.

Whoever pursues the truth lives in the presence of salvation. Without this pursuit, someone must autonomously try to fashion truth through one's own actions. In the pursuit of truth, we can overcome the opposition between orthodoxy and orthopraxis, between the comprehension of truth through thought and the comprehension of truth through faith and love. A Christian's existence and the church's mission necessarily involve participation in the eschatological and historical process of freedom. This participation includes the celebration in the liturgy and the sacraments of the existence of human freedom as well the growing consciousness of the social-historical conditions of oppression and enslavement. Also, there is the challenge of preaching, catechesis, and forms of education as well as the public protest against oppression. Through this involvement, there is solidarity with poor people and with their personal development so that these people take their destiny into their own hands, shaping their own lives and freeing themselves from social compulsions.

The liberating actions of people in poverty, their solidarity with one another, and their class conflict with people of wealth do not necessarily lead, except in extreme cases, to armed uprisings against the people who exploit them. The attaining of freedom primarily comes about as people meet in self-help groups, accept their political and cultural responsibilities, join in volunteer service, and are active in the organizations affiliated with their work and the organizations of their political parties. Men and women engage in these activities in order to accomplish through their power as poor people an entire societal transformation even in relation to global economic structures.

In this regard, the Second Vatican Council speaks of the role of the church insofar as the church becomes the sacrament of freedom in participation with God's historical process of humanization. In *Gaudium et spes* 1, the council states: "The joys and hopes, the grief and anguish of the people of our time, especially of those who are poor or afflicted, are the joys and hopes, the grief and anguish of the followers of Christ as well." Moreover, Vatican II goes on to state in *Gaudium et spes* 4:

> In every age, the church carries the responsibility for reading the signs of the times and of interpreting them in the light of the Gospel. . . . We must be aware of and understand the aspirations, the yearnings, and the often dramatic features of the

world in which we live. . . . Ours is a new age of history with profound and rapid changes spreading gradually to all corners of the earth. They are the products of people's intelligence and creative activity, but they recoil upon them, upon their judgments and desires, both individual and collective, upon their ways of thinking and acting in regard to people and things. We are entitled then to speak of a real social and cultural transformation whose repercussions are felt at the religious level also.

A careful reading of liberation theology reveals that this theology stands entirely in continuity with classical theology, while it simultaneously initiates some basic orientations that were inconspicuously at work in classical theology. One such orientation is expressed in the new language concerning Latin America's actual social situation and its ties to the domination of the world's economic centers of power.

A Critique of Liberation Theology: Its Merits and Limits

The liberation theology of Latin America is totally rejected only by a few theologians, at least when we disregard the concerns of the people who fear for their privileges in society, in the state, and even to some degree in the church. Only specific theoretical elements in liberation theology receive a critical appraisal from the magisterium and theology. One criticism in particular is that at many points liberation theology needs to make further differentiations.

Within the church, there can be no self-immunization by the theologians of a specific region. When European theology tries to serve as the measure of the theologies in the younger churches, Europeans cannot understand a priori liberation theology. But if this inability were always the case, then every translation of something from outside of a region would be pointless. In dialogue it must be possible to attain an overcoming of possible misunderstandings.

Often the conversation runs aground concerning various interpretations of operative concepts such as socialism, capitalism, and class conflict. It must be a primary hermeneutical rule that, in order to resolve problematic aspects of different concepts, theologians must not proceed out of their own system of conceptual relationships. They must inquire into these concepts apart from their implications, and they must take for granted a theology's mediating principles and consequences as the goal of the whole endeavor.

The chief point of concern is always liberation theology's social-analytic reflection and its partial use of Marxist concepts such as the theory of dependence, the scheme of theory and praxis, the interpretation of human beings as the creative shapers of history and the personal subjects in social processes. There should exist no doubt concerning the appropriateness of empirical, social-scientific analysis of human existence as the starting point of theology. Even classical theology begins with the presentation of the situation of human beings whom classical theology regards as created by God and as graced or sinful. Liberation theology extends this line of thought concerning grace and sin into the structural conditions of created existence.

Whether dependence theory provides a complete clarification of the historical situation of the nations of the Third World remains an unresolved issue. Certainly someone can always point to the elusive complexity of factors out of which the present situation is constituted. However, this complexity should not function as an excuse for a lack of thought or action to improve the present situation, for such a lack of thought or action means the preservation of the existing [unjust] relationships. Moreover, in the nations and business centers of North America and Europe there are no alternative theories that can clarify more accurately the phenomena and the factors of exploitation, poverty, and oppression and, hence, that can generate a strategy for a true transformation.

Of course, the actual forms of socialism have historically exhausted themselves. Yet, the validity of specific sociological and economic insights into the system of modern industrial institutions, as these insights are brought to expression by Marx, has not expired. Moreover, these insights are not inseparable from Marxism's atheistic view of human beings. In this atheistic perspective, human beings should be the sovereign creators of their own existence, and, if they are to attain their rightful freedom, human beings must deny the existence of a creator God and also the encompassing action of God's grace. However, Marxism's so-called historical materialism is not a construct sui generis. Many of its theoretical elements are to be examined in relation to their origins in the Jewish-Christian understanding of history and the eschaton.

Christian faith surely does not hold a notion of history as a simply harmonious, ever-evolving reality. It perceives grace and sin at work in the antagonistic, moving interaction in the historical drama. According to liberation theology, grace and sin find a form of expression today in the social opposition between oppression and freedom in Latin America and in the world.

An understanding of the antagonistic drama of history can be made plausible on the basis of rigorous theological reflection. A transcendent reality constitutes history in its beginning and its end. It establishes therefore history in a protological and eschatological frame of reference. And only if human beings are seen to be persons in relation to the absolute responsibility of God, who is history's source and goal, then human beings are also viewed as collaborators in history. For men and women take themselves seriously as actors with responsibilities when, on the basis of their free acceptance of grace, they affirm the objective process of history. When they refuse to do so, they fail to see the goal of history and thus the actualization of human beings in God.

People should not be suspicious of liberation theology in all of its forms simply because of its use of some Marxist ideas. Instead, they should investigate Marxism as an appropriation and secularization of the basic convictions of the Christian theology of history and eschatology. It would be worthwhile to discuss the extent to which liberation theology is the rediscovery of original Christian ideas that are evident when one is able to avoid Marxism's onerous vocabulary. In any case, liberation theology fundamentally differentiates itself from Marxism on the basis of its foundation in a theological anthropology. Liberation theology is truly theology, and, as such, it clearly makes use of the scholarship of sociology, political science, and economics in order to develop its theological themes.

With regard to liberation theology's understanding of history, it is important to discuss the suspicion of its horizontal or this-worldly hope of salvation. There exists the view that liberation theology has in fact adopted the goal of paradise on earth. To be sure, liberation theology rightly objects to a dualism between the other-worldly, future salvation, on the one hand, and this-worldly well-being, on the other. Is liberation theology, as it is actually undertaken, inclined to a monism in which profane history and salvation history, human activity and divine grace, are formed into one without distinction? If earthly well-being—such as nourishment, clothing, housing, education, justice, and liberation—is identical with salvation and if the history of a place is its identity, then this monism runs either toward making something immanent into what we hope for in salvation or toward making a theocratic-totalitarian claim for the promotion of a political-social process.

In order to understand liberation theology properly on this matter, it is helpful to consider the *nouvelle théologie* of the 1950s in France, where Gustavo Gutiérrez studied, and also the theology of grace in Germany, especially that of Karl Rahner. Through this consideration, one arrives at an understanding of the twofold goal of human beings.

There is not, as Neo-Scholasticism holds, an immanent actualization of a human being in this earthly life, on the one side, and, on the other, an unrelated supernatural-transcendent actualization of this individual, an actualization that has absolutely nothing to do with human nature in this life and that is simply added by God extrinsically to a human being after death. By means of this theory of grace as a super-addition to human nature, Neo-Scholastic scholars wanted to secure the nature of freedom and the unrequired character of grace in relation to what is proper to human nature.

However, someone may proceed, as Thomas Aquinas did, on the basis of a divinely intended goal of human beings who possess, in Thomas's words, "a natural yearning for the living God" (*desiderium naturale ad vivendum Deum*). Given this innate orientation, the human nature created by God for eventual union with God finds its self-actualization only in God. In this perspective, human beings are eligible to experience the one salvation in its transcendent and its immanent dimensions.

Nevertheless, earthly well-being and eternal salvation do not come together without differentiation. Eternal salvation is God who communicates God's self with human beings, during this [earthly] time in their lives of faith, and this self-communication is fully realized in their vision of God [after death]. Earthly goods such as freedom, human dignity, justice, and the overcoming of hunger and need are signs, actualizations, and realizations of the one salvation of human beings and humanity on their way in history to the eschaton. There is neither a pure separation nor a simple identification between earthly well-being and eternal salvation. Salvation is a differentiated unity of two interrelated aspects that are dynamically drawn together in the historical and eschatological arena and reciprocally illumine each other.

This relationship [of unity-in-difference] shows itself in the relationship of profane history and salvation history. Certainly world history is not simply the self-objectification of God, as Hegel held. World history is primarily the entire arena of the dramatic movements of the dialectical powers of grace and freedom, on the one side, and sin and oppression, on the other side. However, world history in its innermost kernel is nevertheless salvation history because God, who is the creator/savior of the world and of human beings, has established union with God as the objective goal of the historical movement of men and women and also the goal of their efforts for human liberation.

Thus, whoever engages in groups that work for liberation stands on the side of the divine liberator. In praxis, these men and women undertake the transforming engagement in the historical process toward history's transcendent and immanent goal. In a sense, whoever is active for liberation stands already on God's side, whether this individual is aware of it or not. It is with these individuals that the explicitly believing Christians can collaborate, even though Christians cannot pray, confess belief, and celebrate the Eucharist with these men and women because they are still formally and consciously lacking an explicit, personal relationship to God in Christ as expressed in the confession of faith and through participation in the liturgy.

However, when Christians are with people who claim to be Christian and yet work against liberation and hence against God, they cannot collaborate with these opponents of liberation, nor can they confess their Christian faith with them. Further, they should not celebrate the Eucharist together because serious sin not only excludes one from the Eucharist but also closes one to the Eucharist's content and meaning, to its celebration of grace and liberation. This refusal to join in the Eucharist has nothing to do with a so-called social-class Eucharist, as some critics allege. This refusal should be thought of not in relation to Christians who belong to different social strata but in relation to people who actively and deliberately exploit and oppress other people. Such individuals are excommunicated in the classical sense of the word. That is, the church distances these individuals from its community with the hope that they may undergo a change of heart and be reconciled as a sign of conversion into the church. This reconciliation is subsequently expressed in the communal celebration of the Eucharist.

To sum up, we can understand liberation theology on the whole to be a socially applied *nouvelle théologie*, as formulated by Henri de Lubac, or, also to be a theology of grace, as developed by Karl Rahner, now applied to history and society.

When liberation theology is set in relation to the theologies of de Lubac and Rahner, questions about it and objections to it resolve themselves. One can show that the roots of liberation theology originate in biblical revelation and in the church's theological and magisterial tradition. At this time, liberation theology is likely moving into a further stage of development in the work of individual theologians and in their reflections on the situation in Latin America. Also, it may be burdened at times by some of its representatives' theological weaknesses and their outlandish statements that attract the attention of the media. These issues do not call into question, however, the significant insights of liberation theology.

Concerning contemporary challenges to church life and also to theology, it must be said that the Third-World church and also the world church cannot refuse the further development and application of liberation theology. Through liberation theology, Catholic theology is able to resolve around the world and in our epoch the dualistic dilemma between what is this-worldly and what is other-worldly, between earthly well-being and heavenly salvation—the dualistic dilemma to which there is unfortunately often a monistic solution of subsuming one aspect into the other. This is the dualistic dilemma that Marxism did not produce but surely spoke about. It is not inappropriate to see liberation theology as a radical alternative to the Marxist view of human beings as well as to Marxist talk about a utopia in history.

The methodological claim of liberation theology, with its transforming praxis, is nothing other than a new formulation of the originating event of theology in general. First comes discipleship to Christ, and from this discipleship comes a formulation of the confession that actually concerns Jesus.

Liberation theology may have suffered by engaging the general public in its interests. Yet, even with its unresolved issues, it performs an indispensable contribution to the church's transformative, reflective, and pastoral service. The liberation theology of Latin America is irreplaceable, not only in its regional context but also in its worldwide communication of theology.

—Translated by Robert A. Krieg

CHAPTER 5

Where Will the Poor Sleep? [1]

GUSTAVO GUTIÉRREZ

A series of events in the past few years (economic, political, cultural, and ecclesial) have given us a rough outline—in a surprisingly short period—of a situation that is very new. It has been called a new era, even though we don't yet have the historical distance necessary to name it in any definitive way. But there is no doubt about the unprecedented nature of the present state of things.

I'm talking about a situation that leads us to reconsider many things. A fair number of analyses and proposals made in recent years are now out of date, and numerous discussions and clarifications of an earlier time do not respond fully to current challenges. To ignore these changes would mean locking ourselves in the past, living nostalgically, and condemning ourselves to living with our backs turned to the people of today.[2] This is not a question of being frivolously "up to date" but rather a serious question of the solidarity and service we owe to others. In addition, for a Christian, this means being open to what the Lord wishes to tell us through historical events

---

1. First published in *El rostro de Dios en la historia* (Lima: Universidad Católica, Instituto Bartolomé de Las Casas, CEP, 1996) 9-69.

2. For a comprehensive presentation and analysis of this time, see E. Hobsbawm, "Towards the Millennium," in *Age of Extremes: The Short Twentieth Century, 1914–1991* (London: Michael Joseph, 1994) 558-85. For the author the twenty-first century began in 1992.

that must be read and interpreted, following John XXIII and the Council, as signs of the times.

We cannot avoid an examination of the characteristics that are beginning to define this age. This entails an openness and a willingness to listen. At the same time, and, given our task of proclaiming the reign of God and speaking about faith, we need to analyze the new situation from within a commitment to the gospel. I will attempt this very concretely beginning with the preferential option for the poor, which is a core issue in the theology of liberation.

A brief passage in the book of Exodus can illuminate this proposal for us. Among the commandments that Moses receives from Yahweh to be transmitted to his people, we find—in simple and expressive terms—the one that says we must be concerned about where those who have nothing with which to cover themselves will sleep (cf. Exodus 22:26). The text invites us to ask a question that helps us see what is at stake at the present moment: where are the poor going to sleep in this world which is coming to be and which has, in a certain sense, already taken its first steps? What is going to happen to God's favorites in the time to come?

In the world of the technological and information revolution, of the "globalization" of the economy, of neoliberalism and so-called postmodernism, is there room for those who today are poor and marginalized and who are seeking ways to free themselves from an inhuman state that tramples on their status as human persons and as children of God? What is the role of the gospel and the faith of the poor in a time that is allergic to certainties and to human solidarity? What does the preferential option for the poor mean as a path to integral liberation? Naturally, I can only begin an attempt to respond to the challenges of the present moment.

Theology and the Proclamation of the Gospel

Faith is a gift. To receive this gift means putting oneself behind Jesus as he walks, putting his teachings into practice, and proclaiming the reign of God. The act of faith stands at the beginning of all theology. Reflecting on faith is something that arises spontaneously in a believer; it's a reflection that is motivated by a desire to make one's faith-life deeper and more faithful. But this reflection is not only an individual matter; faith is always lived in community. Both dimensions—the personal and the communitarian—mark our living out of the faith as much as our understanding of it.

The theological task is supported and exercised in the heart of the ecclesial community. It is at the service of the evangelizing mission of the church. This location and this aim give it its meaning and a rough idea of its scope.[3] Theology is a speaking about God animated by faith; God is, in fact, the first and the last theme of theological language.[4] Many other points may be touched on by theology, but this only occurs to the degree that they are related to God.

Theological formulations are always inadequate. We must be ready to take new roads, refine our ideas, modify the way we approach problems. Because of this, we have a diversity of approaches—within the unity of the church's faith—to the revealed Word in the course of history. Indeed, faith cannot be identified with any particular theology, as the traditional saying goes. The various efforts at understanding faith are useful and fruitful but only on condition that none of them sees itself as the only valid one. The meaning and the scope of these reflections require a clear awareness of the modest contribution that they offer to the primary tasks of the church.

Theological reflection takes place first of all, as I said, in service to Christian life and to the evangelizing mission of the ecclesial community; and through this, it also represents a service to humanity. The church exists in the world and must proclaim in accessible and challenging language both the actual presence of the reign of God at this point in historical evolution as well as its future and complete arrival. This perspective is one of the central axes of the Second Vat-

---

3. See G. Gutiérrez, "Teología: una función eclesial," *Páginas* 130 (1994) 10-17. (See chap. 1 in the present volume.)

4. Thomas Aquinas recalled this with conviction and clarity. See *Summa theologicae* I q. 1, a. 7.

ican Council. The acquisition of an appropriate language presupposes an immersion in the desires and needs of human beings (see *Gaudium et spes* 44). In this mission Christians' commitment and theological reflection play a major role.

To evangelize is to proclaim salvation in Christ through words and deeds. Having conquered at their root the forces of sin that control the "old person," the Son of God made flesh, through his surrender to the point of death and his resurrection by the Father, eases the way for "new persons" so that they may fulfill their call to communion with God in the Pauline "face to face" (1 Corinthians 13).

But precisely because this liberation from sin goes to the very heart of human existence, where the freedom of each person in the final analysis either accepts or rejects the gratuitous and redeeming love of God, nothing is outside of the salvific action of Jesus Christ. This action reaches and puts its stamp on every human dimension, personal and social.

Theologies necessarily bear the mark of the time and ecclesial context in which they are born. They continue to live as long as the conditions in which they were born remain substantially in force.[5] Naturally, the great theologies manage to overcome, in some way, chronological and cultural boundaries; less significant ones—no matter how important they may have been in their time—are more subject to time and circumstances. I am referring, of course, to the particular characteristics of a theology (its immediate stimuli, its instruments of analysis, its philosophical notions, and others) and not to the fundamental affirmations that concern revealed truths. The history of theology clearly illustrates what I've just pointed out.

On the other hand, we must also observe that all theological reflection, even with its limits and deficiencies, its passions and inconclusive attempts, enters into dialogue with other efforts to understand faith. What is proper to theology is the help it provides

---

5. People sometimes talk about contextual theologies as if they were a special kind of faith-understanding. It depends on what one means because, in a certain way, all theology is contextual although this does not mean calling into question what is permanent in theological effort.

in elucidating believers' consciousness concerning their encounter with God and what the Good News implies for the Christian community and for the world. Every theology does this with its own resources and its own limitations; it is also enriched by the contribution of other theologies and contributes to them. The most important thing for any faith discourse is not to go on existing, and even less to survive, but rather to carry its waters to wider and mightier rivers, to the life of the church as a whole.

For all these reasons, the sufferings and the anguish, the joys and the hopes of the people of today, as well as the current situation of the church's evangelizing task, should be of more concern to us than the present or future state of a particular theology.

In the Perspective of the Theology of Liberation

Naturally, everything said above about the function of faith discourse in general applies to any particular effort. This is the case with the theology of liberation. As an understanding of faith, it was born in a precise place and at a precise time, seeking to respond to historical situations that by their nature were in flux and that both challenged and opened new avenues for the church's evangelizing task. As an effort at understanding required by the gift of faith, theology is therefore permanent, and, at the same time, it is always changing inasmuch as it responds to concrete questions and to a given cultural world.

AN EVANGELICAL GUIDELINE

As is well known, since its beginnings liberation theology, born out of a deep pastoral concern, has been tied to the life of the church, to its documents, to its communal celebration, to its concern for preaching the gospel, and to its liberating commitment to Latin American society, in particular to the poorest of its members. The Latin American bishops' conferences of those decades (Medellín, Puebla, Santo Domingo), numerous texts by national conferences of bishops, and other documents corroborate this claim, even when they invite us to make a critical discernment in the face of unfounded assertions and positions that some claimed they could deduce from liberation theology.

Along the lines of the theme that I have proposed to deal with here, I would like to emphasize certain aspects of the contribution made by the life and reflection of the Latin American church with a view to the future.

The fundamental contribution of liberation theology, it seems to me, revolves around what is called "the preferential option for the poor." This option shapes, deepens, and in the end corrects many commitments made during those years as well as the theological reflections linked to them. The option for the poor is radically rooted in the gospel and thus constitutes an important guideline for sifting through the fast-paced events and the intellectual currents of our days.

John XXIII's proposal regarding "the church of all and especially the church of the poor"[6] found fertile ground in Latin America and the Caribbean. Our continent is the only one where the majority of the population is both poor and Christian. The reality of massive and inhuman poverty led us to ask about the biblical significance of poverty. Toward the middle of the 1960s the distinction among three meanings of the term "poor" was formulated in the theological field: first, *real* poverty (often called material poverty) as a scandalous state of things, not willed by God; second, *spiritual* poverty as spiritual childhood, one expression of which (but not the only one) is detachment from the things of this world; and poverty as a *commitment* in solidarity with the poor and in protest against poverty.

Medellín authoritatively picked up this distinction ("Poverty," no. 4), and it thus acquired an enormous reach in the world of the Latin American church and beyond it. This focus inspired the commitment and reflection of many Christian communities and, as Puebla approached, became the foundation of what, in the texts of that bishops' conference, would be denoted with the phrase "prefer-

---

6. Radio address of September 11, 1962.

ential option for the poor." In fact, in this expression's three terms, we find, one by one, the three notions distinguished by Medellín. Later, the Santo Domingo conference would reaffirm this option in which we should find inspiration "for every evangelizing action, communitarian and personal" (no. 178).

This option recalls and takes up once again a penetrating biblical line of thought that, in one way or another, was always present in the Christian world.[7] At the same time the present formulation gives it a new force in today's circumstances; it has made its way forward and is now found in the universal ecclesiastical magisterium. John Paul II referred to it on numerous occasions. Let me mention only two. First, in *Centesimus annus* (CA), he affirms that "re-reading" *Rerum novarum* in the light of contemporary realities allows us to observe that it is "an excellent testimony of the continuity within the Church of what today is called 'the preferential option for the poor'" (no. 11).[8] And in his later letter *Tertio millennio adveniente* (TMA), of special interest to me here, the pope recalls that Jesus came to preach the Good News to the poor (in reference to Matthew 11:5 and Luke 7:22) and asks, "How can we fail to lay greater emphasis on the *Church's preferential option for the poor and the outcast?*" (no. 51).

PREFERENCE AND GRATUITOUSNESS

The topic of poverty and marginalization invites us to speak about justice and to keep in mind the Christian's duties in this regard. This in fact is what we have done, and this focus is fruitful without a

---

7. See for example, in the case of the Methodist churches, Theodore W. Jennings, *Good News to the Poor: John Wesley's Evangelical Economics* (Nashville: Abingdon Press, 1990).

8. The text continues: "an option which in *Sollicitudo rei socialis* [SRS] is defined as 'a special form of primacy in the exercise of Christian charity (no. 42)'" (CA, 11). For an overview of the presence of the option for the poor in the social teaching of the church, see Donal Dorr, *Option for the Poor: A Hundred Years of Vatican Social Teaching* (Dublin: Gill & Macmillan; New York: Orbis Books, 1983).

doubt. But we should not lose sight of what makes the preferential option for the poor such a central issue. At the root of this option is the gratuitousness of God's love. This is the ultimate foundation of the preference.[9]

The term "preference" itself rules out all exclusivity and aims to stress those who should be the first—not the only—persons in our solidarity. In commenting on the meaning of preference in my theological work, I have frequently spoken of the great challenge coming from the need to maintain the universality of God's love and, at the same time, God's predilection for those who are the last ones in history. To stay with just one of these two extremes is to deform the gospel message.

In the final analysis it is important to stress that the option for the poor is an option for the God of the kingdom proclaimed to us by Jesus. The definitive reason for our commitment to the poor thus is not found in the social analysis that we use, nor in the direct experience we might have of poverty, nor in our human compassion. These are all valid motives which no doubt play a significant role in our lives and solidarities. However, for us as Christians this commitment is fundamentally based on our faith in the God of Jesus Christ. It is a *theocentric option* that is prophetic and is rooted in the gratuitous love of God. It is also required by this gratuitousness. And there is nothing more demanding, as we know, than gratuitousness (see the letter of Paul to Philemon 21).

The poor person has priority not because he or she is necessarily better than others from the moral or religious point of view, but because God is God. The entire Bible is stamped by God's loving predilection for the weak and mistreated of human history. The gospel beatitudes sharply reveal this to us as they tell us that the preference for the poor, the hungry, and the suffering is grounded in the gratuitous goodness of the Lord.[10] The preferential option for

---

9. For this reason, and for others that will be mentioned in what follows, the term "preference" has a key role in the phrase that I am discussing.

10. This point is treated with all possible clarity by Jacques Dupont, *Les béatitudes* (3 vols.) (Paris: Gabalda, 1964-1969). Along the same lines, see

the poor thus is not merely a pastoral guideline or a perspective for theological reflection. It is also, and in the first place, a spiritual path in the strong sense of that expression. It is a journey of encounter with God and with the gratuitousness of God's love, a walking "in the presence of the Lord in the land of the living" (Psalm 116:9). If we don't go to this depth of spirituality, of following Jesus—that is, to the very heart of Christian life—we cannot perceive the scope and fruitfulness of this option.

A philosopher of profound biblical (and Talmudic) roots has developed a line of thinking, or more concretely an ethic (for him ethics is the primary philosophy), about alterity that might illumine what is under consideration here. I'm referring to Emmanuel Levinas.[11] "The Bible," he tells us, "is about the priority of the other in relation to the I." What is true for all persons becomes even more radical in the case of the poor. "In the other," he continues, "I always see the widow and the orphan. The other always goes before me."[12] The widow, the orphan, and the stranger constitute a trilogy that in the Bible denotes the poor. Letting the other go first arises from the other's very status as other; this is true even when the other is unaware of me or looks at me with indifference. It is not a question of reciprocity; we are faced with the primacy of the other, which leads to what Levinas calls "the dissymmetry of the interpersonal relationship"[13] or "ethical asymmetry." Theologically I would say that if the other, and in an even more demanding way, the poor, ought to go first, it is because of gratuitousness, because we must love as God loves. This means giving not as compensation for what one has received but rather because one loves. "God loved us first," John tells us (1 John 4:19). To be a Christian is to respond to this initiative.

Jacques Schlosser, *Le règne de Dieu dans les dits de Jésus* (Paris: Gabalda, 1980).

11. In this perspective of alterity, and in relation to the parable of the Good Samaritan, I cited Levinas in *Teología de la liberación* (Lima: CEP, 1971, 1988 [2nd ed.]) 251 and 309 respectively.

12. *De Dieu qui vient à l'idée* (Paris: Vrin, 1982) 145.

13. Ibid.

There can be no doubt that this is a demanding ethic. For the Christian the relation to the other becomes even deeper when we consider our faith in the Incarnation and are attentive to its repercussions.[14] The Bible stresses the link between love for God and love for neighbor; in various ways it tells us that to mistreat the poor person is to offend God. This idea is affirmed in the Gospels and culminates with the Matthean text of the final judgment (25:31-46). One's action toward the poor is directed to Christ himself. As Puebla says, in the "very concrete faces" of the poor we must "recognize the suffering features of Christ the Lord who questions and challenges us" (no. 31).[15] The Christian life proceeds between grace and exigency.

This deeply biblical concern maintains with great clarity the distinction between God and the human being but does not separate them. Commitment to the poor is not limited to the social realm, though it is present there of course. But solidarity also includes as something primordial a profoundly spiritual content and a christological foundation. It has a close and indissoluble relation with the basic truths of our faith. Only against this backdrop can we appreciate the meaning of the preferential option for the poor. This is how many Christians in Latin America have lived it out, and are living it out today. It thus turns out to be an overriding and fruitful guideline for understanding, through the lens of faith, the times in which we are living.[16]

---

14. We are now on a level that is different from the strictly philosophical. Levinas takes up, in a profound way, the challenging question that comes to us from the "face of the other" (see *Totalité e infini* [The Hague: M. Nijhoff, 1961] 168-94). But naturally he does not relate the other to the Incarnation of the Son of God, which is outside of his horizon.

15. This idea was taken up again and deepened at Santo Domingo (nos. 178-79).

16. Juan Carlos Scannone has demonstrated the fecundity of this point of view in philosophical work. See "La irrupción del pobre y la pregunta filosófica en América Latina," in *Irrupción del pobre y quehacer filosófico* (Buenos Aires: Bonum, 1993) 123-40.

Toward a Planetary Economy

A common theme these days is what is called the "globalization" of the economy. In a certain way, the road to a single world was taken by humanity in the last few centuries, but today this feature is more prominent.

A Fascinating and Cruel Century

Enrique Iglesias, president of the Inter-American Development Bank, once said that the coming century would be "a fascinating and cruel century." Like all somewhat paradoxical phrases, this one seems challenging and attractive. However, if we make the effort to examine it more closely, it reveals the tragic reality that it expresses.

Indeed, thanks to the extraordinary development of science and technology, a fascinating era has begun. The possibilities for communication (or at least the sharing of information) among persons such as humanity has never before known as well as the capacity for dominating nature that goes beyond our planet's limits make real what only a short time ago seemed like science fiction. To this must be added the unlimited opportunities for consumption and also, unfortunately, the potential for destruction that could affect the entire human race. As human beings and as believers, we must not fail to appreciate and admire these advances despite the storm clouds that can also be made out on the horizon.

Nevertheless, at this particular moment the future looks as if it will be fascinating for those who have a certain social standing and who take part in cutting-edge technological knowledge. Those who have this chance tend to form an international human stratum closed in on itself, forgetting about those who are not part of their club, including some in their own countries.

The latter are the poor. The second adjective of the phrase applies primarily to them. The coming century will indeed be cruel for the "insignificant" of history. Their poverty and marginalization will increase unless we make an enormous effort at solidarity, and there will be greater misery and those who live in misery will be ever more numerous, as the indices of all international organizations show in this regard.

In other words, the immediate future will not, in truth, be fascinating and cruel for the same persons. This makes more urgent the challenge of our time and more demanding the question put to faith in the God of Jesus Christ, who loves all and calls on us to protect the smallest.

A MARKET WITHOUT RESTRICTIONS

We live in a time that is more and more dominated by the liberal economy, or neoliberal if you prefer. A market without restrictions, called to regulate itself on its own, has become the nearly absolute principle of economic life. The famous and classic *laissez-faire* of the early liberal economy universally suggests today—in theory at least—that any intervention of political power aimed at regulating the market, or even dealing with social necessities, works to the detriment of economic growth and ends up hurting everyone. Thus, if problems arise in economic development, the market is the only solution.

After some ups and downs,[17] the liberal wave has recently

---

17. The "savage capitalism" of earlier times caused a reaction by workers, "justified from the point of view of social morality" (*Laborem exercens* 8), who organized to protect their rights. It was strongly criticized for its ruthless character in the name of principles and human and religious realities that placed the value of the human person at the center of the economy (cf. the church's social teaching). It also endured harassment by socialist movements that sought to orient workers' organizations ideologically. And it confronted the great crisis of 1929 very badly. One of the results of these situations and debates was what is known as the social welfare state, which tried to alleviate some of the greatest problems in the application of economic neoliberalism but which never really managed to be set up in poor countries. The great neoliberal economists (Hayek, Friedman, and others) in turn launched an energetic critique of the social welfare state which had begun to experience economic difficulties. See the sharp analysis of Albert Hirschman, *The Rhetoric of Reaction* (Cambridge, MA: Belknap Press, 1991). At the moment we face a return to the original postulates of capitalism with all the strength that comes

regained its momentum and is now growing without restraint. Large transnational corporations (the dominant feature of the present economic order) and rich countries pressure poor countries to open their markets, privatize their economies, and carry out what are called structural adjustments. International organizations (such as the World Bank and the International Monetary Fund) have been effective agents in this integration of weak economies into a single market. An awareness of interdependence can in itself be a good thing, but the form it takes today is one of an asymmetry that underlines the existing unjust inequality.[18] The new element in the globalization of the economy is financial capital that crosses borders as it sails around the world with incredible maneuverability in pursuit of new and greater profit. National economies—even those of large countries—get blurred.[19]

One aspect of this globalization, and one of the most painful and pressing aspects for poor countries, is the foreign debt that keeps debtor nations weighed down and prostrate. If this matter does not receive an appropriate and immediate solution, there is little chance that poor countries will be able to get out of the situation they are in today.[20]

Various factors have intervened in the process that has led to this result. Let me mention two. On the political level the fall of authoritarian socialism in Russia and in the countries of Eastern Europe has certainly been of great importance. It refused to see the complex

---

from the universal dimensions it has acquired. This has special consequences for poor nations.

18. The situation is so clear that despite his defense of the market, the managing director of the International Monetary Fund himself recognized that we cannot "ignore the potential crushing of the weak and neglected" that results from market competition in the circumstances of the world today (Michel Camdessus, "Economía ¿para qué futuro?" *La cuestión social* 4, no. 1 [1996] 67).

19. On the matter of national economies and the global economy, see Robert B. Reich, *The Work of Nations* (New York: Vintage Books, 1992).

20. See Javier Iguíñiz, *Deuda externa en América Latina: Exigencias éticas desde la doctrina social de la iglesia* (Lima: CEP, IBC, 1995).

dimensions of the human being and systematically violated the right to liberty.[21] From a bipolar world we have moved to a unipolar one, more politically and militarily than economically, to tell the truth. The other factor and one of longer-standing inspiration, is the role played by technological knowledge (for example, new materials, new sources of energy, biotechnology), one of whose most dynamic aspects concerns information.[22] This development has brought notable changes to the production process. Furthermore, it is also more and more obvious today that knowledge has become the most important axis of accumulation in economic activity. Advances in this field have allowed people to press down on the accelerator of insatiable exploitation—and depredation—of the planet's natural resources, which are a patrimony belonging to all of humanity. And this in turn has made us see the gravity of the ecological question in our time.

With their achievements and abuses, their advances and cruelties, their possibilities and oversights, the outlook for our contemporary economy and social fabric today has changed in recent years at a dizzying pace, as has not happened in centuries. This new situation calls for the renewal of analytical methods capable of accounting for the multiplicity of factors in play in the social and economic framework of our time.[23] But this situation also invites us to analyze

---

21. This event opened new space on the international level, but "the existing situations of injustice and oppression" have not been automatically eliminated (CA 26; see also 42).

22. In this regard people have spoken of a third revolutionary wave in the history of humanity. The theme has been popularized by the works of Alvin and Heidi Toffler. See also Taichi Sakaiya, *Historia del futuro: la sociedad del conocimiento* (Santiago de Chile: Editorial Andrés Bello, 1994). These works have an optimistic tone and are perhaps less attentive to the other side of this knowledge revolution today and its consequences for the poorest sectors of the world's population.

23. Dependency theory (in reality more an attitude or frame of mind than a systematic theory) was present in the early stages of liberation theology in the period dealing with socio-economic reality. Despite its undeniable contributions during the 1970s, we see it today as an inadequate tool used to explain

it through a Christian ethic and by means of theological reflection aimed at making an unavoidable discernment.

ETHICS AND THE ECONOMY

Does ethics, and very concretely, Christian ethics, have anything to say to the economic world?

This question would have made no sense in the sixteenth century. Moral theologians of the time (Francisco de Vitoria among them), who were concerned about the matters raised by nascent capitalism (sometimes called mercantile capitalism), would only be surprised by the question and would say that the answer is obviously affirmative. And in the economic classics of the eighteenth century we still find philosophical and ethical concerns in the new field into which they were venturing.

But little by little the nascent discipline tends to conform to the model and the rationality of the natural sciences and begins to claim its autonomy vis-à-vis politics. It even tries to replace politics; in the end, people think that what is decisive for life in society plays out in the economic sphere. If we take into account the situation of the political world in this regard, we must agree that this is true in the view of the majority of citizens. Politics becomes more and more an arena in which nothing of importance takes place. Thus we see its ever-declining prestige in the world today, and this certainly includes Latin America and the Caribbean.

But there is more: the modern economy challenges commonly accepted moral norms and not only in circles we might call traditional. Envy, selfishness, and greed become the driving forces of the

---

new facts, new forms of dependency, and to tackle the enormous complexity of the present state of things. See the study by Cristóbal Kay, *Latin American Theories of Development and Underdevelopment* (London: Routledge, 1989). But the *fact* of dependency, which in many ways has increased, is one thing, while the *theory* which interpreted that reality at a certain moment is something else. What distinguishes any understanding that seeks to be rigorous, including on the sandy soil of social reality, is its openness to new hypotheses and possibilities.

economy; solidarity and concern for the poorest are seen, by contrast, as obstacles to economic growth and in the end as counterproductive in achieving a situation of well-being from which all persons might benefit one day.

Some clear-eyed economists of the liberal tradition were aware of this disruption of values, but they accepted it because they saw in it something necessary and inevitable. This is the case of John Maynard Keynes, who affirmed with horrifying clarity in a text written between 1928 and 1930 that "when accumulation no longer has such social importance . . . we will be able to free ourselves of many of the pseudo-moral principles that we've had hanging over us for two hundred years. . . . The love of money as a possession will be recognized for what it really is: something unwholesome and unpleasant."[24]

Keynes thought that the moment would come when we would be able to call things by their names and say that "greed is a bad habit, that the practice of usury is a crime, and that the love of money is a detestable thing." But with disillusioned and disturbing resignation he maintains, "Be careful! We are not yet at that moment. For about one hundred years at least we must pretend among ourselves and in front of all others that what is just is bad and what is bad is just." The reason for this inversion of values lies in the fact that "the unjust is useful and the just is not. Greed, usury, and caution have to be our gods for a little longer. In fact only they can lead us through the tunnel of economic need and carry us into the light of day."[25]

---

24. The text continues in very harsh terms: love of money is "one of those semi-pathological inclinations that are put in the hands of specialists in mental illnesses."

25. "Economic Possibilities for Our Grandchildren," in *The Collected Writings: Essays in Persuasion*, vol. IX (3rd ed.; London: Macmillan, 1972) 329, 330, and 331. For an ethical and economic critique of neoliberalism, see, among his other works, M. Douglas Meeks, *God the Economist: The Doctrine of God and Political Economy* (Minneapolis: Fortress Press, 1989); Hugo Assmann and Franz Hinkelammert, *A idolatría do mercado: Um ensaio sobre economía e teología* (Petropolis: Vozes, 1989); J. de Santa Ana, *O amor e as paixões: Crítica teológica à economía política* (Aparecida SP: Editoria Santu-

I have quoted Keynes at some length, and for this I apologize, but these words reveal a great deal about the difficult relationship, to say the least, between ethics and economics in the view of one of the great economists of our time. Although Keynes is seen as a moderate among them, not all liberal thinkers have his acumen and frankness; instead, they don't hesitate to take a stance that derives from the requirements of an economy marked by an aggressively individualistic approach.

This topic is not new and has been addressed on many occasions. The large number of contemporary studies of the issue proves how important it is to deal in depth with the economy from an ethical and theological perspective—and more concretely, beginning with the preferential option for the poor. We must certainly respect the autonomy belonging to a discipline that seeks to understand the field of economic activity in the strictest possible way. There have been many misguided exchanges about this in the past, and we need to learn from that experience. But this does not mean that economics is a field absolutely independent of human existence nor that it is the heart or the whole of it. Economic activity most definitely must be located and analyzed in the context of human life as a whole and in the light of faith. The criterion of immediate efficacy is not decisive.

In 1967 *Populorum progressio* had already posited the need for an "integral development" (nos. 20-21). Pulling together traditional elements of the church's social teaching and going to biblical sources, John Paul II firmly established the cornerstone of a Christian approach: the primacy of the human being over things, from which there flows the priority of work over capital (see *Laborem exercens* passim; the idea had already been presented in *Redemptor hominis* 16).[26]

---

ario, 1989); and Jung Mo Sung, *Deus numa economia sem coração* (São Paulo: Edições Paulinas, 1992).

26. See the commentary by Ricardo Antoncich, *Trabajo y libertad: Reflexiones en torno a la teología de la liberación y a la encíclica sobre el trabajo humano* (Buenos Aires: Latinoamérica Libros, 1988) 76-95. Since 1990

As I have already said, today we see more and more works—and from different regions of the globe—about the ethical norms needed for economic activity and about the religious perversion expressed in certain justifications of an economy centered on unrestricted market forces. These studies recognize the values of liberty, personal initiative, possibilities that open humanity up to technical progress, and even the role that the market can play within certain parameters. But they firmly denounce the logic of a market that humiliates individual persons, whole peoples, and cultures both through its homogenizing zeal and the new social divisions that it provokes. They also question the hypocrisy of an economic liberalism that has no reservations about dictatorships or totalitarian states and readily disconnects economic freedom from other freedoms.[27]

An important task for theological reflection in this field is to spell out which "structures of sin" (SRS 36) there are in the present economic order. That is, which aspects of our socio-economic structures create and maintain unjust inequalities among persons and thus break friendship with God? Sin is not accessible to simple social analysis, but for Christian reflection it is in fact the root of all

---

a body of the United Nations (the United Nations Development Program, or UNDP) has published an Annual Report on Human Development, which seeks "to put the human being in the center of development" (1995 Report, 11). This principle leads us to affirm that human growth is a necessary measure for reaching the goal, which is human development, but is not to be confused with it. To take other human dimensions into account allows human development to renew in a serious and well-supported way the focus of the developed countries and those in the process of development, as well as the strategy for getting out of underdevelopment. See in this regard the well-known works of the economist Amartya Sen.

27. It is important to note that in certain Christian and theological circles one can also find a tendency to look favorably on the liberal economy, in particular in the United States, about which there is an extensive bibliography. See, for example, Michael Novak, *The Spirit of Democratic Capitalism* (New York: Simon & Schuster, 1982).

social injustice. Idolatrous elements, lodged in the fact of, and in the justifications of, the primacy of profit and the absolute character of the market, deserve special attention.

In this context I am particularly concerned with the question of the exclusion of the poorest, now considered irrelevant in the dominant economic system. The following section will deal with this matter.

Destined to Insignificance

The Gospel of Luke offers us a challenging parable from which at this point I would like to cite only two brief lines: "There was a rich man . . ."; "at his gate lay a poor man . . ." (16:19-20).

This is the situation in which humanity finds itself today. Poor nations lie beside rich nations, ignored by the latter; but we have to add that the breach between them is getting wider. The same thing is happening within each country. The world's population is more and more situated at the two extremes of the economic and social spectrum.

On the other hand, and surprisingly, in the Lucan text the poor person has a name: Lazarus; the rich and powerful person, by contrast, does not. In the world today the situation is reversed: the poor are anonymous and seem destined for an even greater anonymity. They are born and die without being noticed. They are disposable pieces in a history that eludes their grasp and excludes them.

Having been thrown into this relationship by the Gospel parable, we can also observe that the poor are not only at the gates of the rich countries. Many poor people struggle to get into rich countries in search of better or simply different living conditions. Migration on this scale is an issue today and poses countless problems in the industrialized nations about which the media inform us every day. Fear and rejection of immigrants, legal or illegal, sometimes has the appearance of racism, which has been criticized by the church a number of times. The issue will perhaps only become more serious in the future.

POVERTY: A CHALLENGE TO THEOLOGY

Liberation theology was born because of the challenge presented to faith by the massive and inhuman poverty of Latin America and the Caribbean.[28] Thus its earliest versions were reflections on the biblical meaning of the different kinds of poverty and a consideration, in the light of faith, of the evangelizing commitment of Christians—and of the entire church—to the poor. Many questions can be asked and issues raised about subsequent developments in this theological current and about the social analysis used to understand the reality of poverty and its causes. But for now, in relation to our theme here, let's simply ask how poverty challenges the Christian conscience today.

The first assertion is that the issue has worsened. The 1996 report of the United Nations Development Program contains disturbing numbers. It concludes that "the world is more and more polarized, and the distance between the poor and the rich gets wider and wider."[29] Something similar is taking place within each country,

---

28. "Inhuman misery" (Medellín, "Poverty," no. 1), "anti-evangelical poverty" (Puebla, no. 1159), "the most devastating and humiliating scourge that Latin America and the Caribbean are experiencing" (Santo Domingo, no. 179).

29. 1996 Report, 2. In the last thirty years the share of income of the poorest 20% of the world's population dropped from 2.3% (already very low) to 1.4%. In contrast the share of the richest 20% increased from 70% to 85%. "That doubled the ratio of the shares of the richest and the poorest—from 30:1 to 61:1" (1996 Report, 2). If we add to this the inequality between rich and poor within countries, the gap between the richest and the poorest of the world seriously widens. The report provides a further impressive fact: the assets of the 358 richest persons in the world "exceed the combined annual incomes of countries with 45% of the world's people" (l.c.). The 1999 Report notes that "the assets of the three top billionaires are more than the combined GNP of all least developed countries and their 600 million people" (1999 Report, 3). Indeed, this report demonstrates that the inequities between rich and poor have grown both within countries as well as on the international level. In the latter case, "one-fifth of the world's population have 86% of GDP—the bottom fifth just 1%" (l.c.).

including the rich nations. This fact and other data reveal that the population living in poverty or extreme poverty is growing both in relative and in absolute terms.[30] The result is horrific: poverty continues to exist and is even deepening.[31] For this reason its challenges to our solidarity and to our thought remain in force today, with even greater urgency and scope.

One expression of this deterioration is what is called economic and social exclusion. This is not a completely new reality or analytical category. In some ways the poor were always excluded and marginalized (think, for example, of the indigenous and black populations in Latin America and the Caribbean). But this must not prevent us from seeing what is different today.[32] The notion of social exclusion has various dimensions. On the economic level, the new means of production, thanks in large part to the knowledge revolution, causes the price of raw materials to decline with consequences in poor countries, and they make access to the labor market dependent on the technical qualifications of the worker. This de facto excludes the great majority of the poor today.[33]

---

30. Let me add that among poor regions Latin America has the greatest inequality in income distribution. See *Informe de la comisión latinoamericana y del Caribe sobre el desarrollo social* (1995).

31. According to a World Bank estimate, the ratio between the income per capita of the richest countries and that of the poorest countries grew from 11:1 in 1870 to 38:1 in 1980 and to 52:1 in 1985 (cited by Javier Iguíñiz, "Conexión y desconexión entre economía y desarrollo humano," in *El rostro de Dios en la historia* [Lima: Universidad Católica, Instituto Bartolomé de Las Casas, CEP, 1996] 71-104). For more on this situation, see the troubling data provided by the World Bank, *World Development Report 2000/2001: Attacking Poverty* (New York: Oxford University Press, 2000).

32. See A. Figueroa, T. Altamirano, D. Sulmont, *Desigualdad y exclusión social en el Perú* (Lima: Instituto internacional de estudios laborales [OIT], 1996).

33. Furthermore, the technification and automation of work tends to dispense with manual labor, and this happens in industrialized countries too. This gives rise to the job crisis (*Laborem exercens* 8 calls it the "plague of unemployment") of our time. This in turn is expressed by the phenomenon of

Exclusion on the political level (which means nonparticipation in decisions made in this sphere) and on the cultural level (discrimination based on race or gender) increases economic exclusion and feeds on it.

These facts are leading to the configuration of humanity into two branches. One of them, that of the excluded, is less and less relevant in the functioning of the world economy and the society that is being more and more firmly established. For this reason I have for a long time referred to the poor as "insignificant" to the extent that their human dignity and their status as sons and daughters of God are not recognized by contemporary society. Furthermore, the term "insignificant" allowed me to recall that for those who believe in the God who does not arbitrarily favor some over others no one can be insignificant.

FROM THE STANDPOINT OF THE LEAST
Inspired by the universal magisterium of the church, the bishops of the United States some years ago proposed a guideline for evaluating a particular political economy. Referring to the option for the poor and to the need to evaluate social and economic activity "from the standpoint of the poor," they affirmed, "if society is to provide justice for *all*, we must recognize the priority of the claims of the marginalized and of those whose rights have been denied."[34] How the weakest are affected is a criterion for deciding whether justice exists in a society.[35]

This is a crucial vantage point, especially if we consider the fact that the marginalized are often the victims of a social and economic

---

economic growth without jobs, which "results in long working hours and very low incomes for hundreds of millions of persons in low productivity work in agriculture and the informal sector," as the UNPD Report puts it (1996, 2).

34. "Economic Justice for All" (1986), no. 87. Emphasis in the text.

35. This criterion brings to mind the second principle of justice in John Rawls (*Teoría de la justicia* [2nd ed.; Mexico: FCE, 1996] 68), with its nuance about the consequences for the poor to which I referred.

system. The Latin American experience made us understand some time ago that, in the final analysis, poverty means death, early and unjust death. By this we do not mean that poverty is not also an economic and social reality. But if we remain at these levels, we do not perceive the radicalness of what is at stake in the issue of poverty: the life and death of persons.

Poverty as we know it in our world today is an all-encompassing question put to every human conscience and to the Christian conception of life. John Paul expressed it passionately during his 1984 visit to Canada in his comments on Matthew 25:31-46, which is very apropos of our topic. "Christ presents himself to us," said the pope, "as a Judge. He has a special right to make this judgment since he became one of us, our brother." The pope then invited us not to stop at an individualistic interpretation of the Christian ethic since it "also has a social dimension." Then, placing the Lord's words in a broad and demanding historical context, he maintained that Christ "is referring to the whole universal dimension of injustice and evil. He is speaking of what today we usually call the North–South divide. Not only East–West but also North–South, with the North richer and richer and the South poorer and poorer." John Paul II then pointed out serious and shocking consequences for rich nations: "In the light of Christ's words, this poor South will judge the rich North. And the poor people and poor nations—poor in different ways, not only lacking food, but also deprived of freedom and other human rights—will judge those people who take these goods away from them, amassing to themselves the imperialistic monopoly of economic and political supremacy at the expense of others."[36]

---

36. Homily during the Mass at the Namao airport (Edmonton, Canada), September 17, 1984, nos. 3-4. Years before in his encyclical *Redemptor hominis* the pope had written about the same Matthean text: "This eschatological scene must always be 'applied' to man's history; it must always be made the 'measure' for human acts" (no. 16).

These words are stern, but they put things on their proper footing. The monumental and definitive scope of the scene on which the pope commented as well as the depth of his commentary helps us see the theological consequences of the theme of poverty. As important as its economic and social dimensions are, they do not exhaust its significance for our reflection, as I said before.[37]

Before concluding this point, it is important to recall that the poor, insignificant and excluded, are not passive persons waiting for someone to extend them a hand. They not only lack things; many human possibilities and riches are bubbling away in them. The poor and marginalized of Latin America often possess a culture with its own eloquent values that come from their race, their history, and their language. They have energies like those seen in women's organizations from one end of the continent to the other, fighting for the lives of their families and of the poor, confronting the crisis with an astonishing inventiveness and creative force.

For a great number of poor people in Latin America, Christian faith has played a critical role as a source of inspiration and a powerful reason for refusing to lose hope in the future. It provides encouragement for a people that proclaims, as a poor squatter did in Lima in front of John Paul II in 1985, "We are hungry for bread and we are hungry for God." In this way he distinguished, without separating, two radical human needs. The pope responded to his greeting in a simple and spirited way: "May your hunger for God remain and your hunger for bread disappear."

The Undermining of Thought

The stage of history into which we are entering is complex. The contemporary mind is shaped not only by economic and political factors but equally by others of a cultural nature. I am referring to what

---

37. Along these same lines we have the challenge that comes in the texts about the faces of the poor that we find in Puebla (nos. 31-39) and Santo Domingo (nos. 178-79).

some people call "postmodernity" or "postmodern thought." I am aware of the ambiguity of the concept, and above all of the term, but it undoubtedly corresponds to an aspect of reality.

It is appropriate to state at the outset that this is not an issue confined to intellectual minorities, although this perspective has more of an impact in those circles. Nor should we think that it is limited to Europe and North America although, once again, it is on those continents where this subject is more widely written about and discussed. The media, art, literature, and certain theologies as well transmit some of its theses beyond the intellectual circles of countries still called Third World, at the same time as they condition many attitudes. Some of its features reinforce neoliberalism's tendency to overlook the insignificant of this world, something I mentioned earlier. Other features, it is true, may open new perspectives on the topic I am addressing.

It is not pointless, then, to set before us the question that will serve as the guiding theme in the following pages: "Where are the poor going to sleep in the postmodern world (or whatever we call it)?" Trying to answer this question will help me sketch the paths to be followed from the point of view of Christian witness.

The Crisis of Modernity

I will not enter into the debate about whether we are in a historical era that we can call postmodern or whether this is a stage of modernity, or more precisely, a vision of it. This matter has been widely discussed, and there is a great variety of opinions on the subject. But as I said above, it is clear that there are aspects of reality that are accentuated by these perspectives and that deserve a certain consideration. There are ambivalences and confusions hard to clear up; nevertheless, there are also silhouettes that suggest a particular moment in the history of thought and of daily human behavior that for convenience I'll call "postmodern."

What we face here is a reaction against some of the great themes of modernity—concretely, against what representatives of this school of thought call the "great narratives" (or "metanarratives") proper to modernity.[38] J. F. Lyotard outlines them as follows: "the progressive emancipation of reason and of liberty, the progressive or catastrophic emancipation from work (the source of alienated value in capitalism), prosperity for all of humanity through the advance of capitalist techno-science." The author adds—and this is important for my purpose here—"and also, if Christianity is included within modernity (opposed, therefore, to ancient classicism), the salvation of creatures by means of the conversion of souls via the mystical account of martyr love."[39]

A direct rejection is made of "Hegel's philosophy [which] totalizes these narratives and, in that sense, concentrates speculative modernity in itself."[40] For this author a philosophy of history is always involved in the legitimation of knowledge by means of a metanarrative.[41] What he rejects is the will to power that the great narratives of modernity represent. Moreover, postmodern people see in this attitude a type of violence that robs individuals of their freedom and thus must be rejected.

Alluding to Weber's famous analysis of modernity as disenchantment of the world (or its desacralization) produced by the new rationality, postmodernity has been spoken of as "disillusionment with disillusionment." There is, indeed, a frustration about modernity, for it seems not to have fulfilled its promises. Instead of social peace, rational and transparent behaviors, and personal happiness, we have had devastating wars, political instability, and terrible explosions of violence. Auschwitz is cited as a paradigmatic example of the inhumanity against which postmodernity is reacting. Many advances

---

38. "Simplifying in the extreme, 'postmodern' may be considered incredulity regarding metanarratives"; see J. F. Lyotard, *La condition postmoderne* (Paris: Editions de Minuit, 1979) 7.

39. J. F. Lyotard, *La postmodernidad explicada a los niños* (Barcelona: Gedisa, 1987) 29.

40. Ibid.

41. Lyotard, *La condition postmoderne*, 7. In this sense Marxism should be considered one of these metanarratives.

in science and technology have become instruments of destruction.

Every unitary concept of history is therefore out of bounds.[42] It doesn't make sense to organize the events of the human world under the idea of a universal history of humanity and a history whose development is to a certain extent known ahead of time. We only have small accounts, individual and local histories. There are no metaphysical foundations of historical development. We are facing what has been called the fragmentation of human knowledge.

Part of the same basic movement but with some differences from Lyotard, G. Vattimo thinks that "it is a matter of considering and assessing what the dissolution of foundational thought entails, namely, the dissolution of metaphysics."[43] Inspired by Nietzsche and Heidegger, he proposes what he calls "weak thought" and specifies that "this is not a school of thought about weakness but rather about diminution. It recognizes a path of dissolution in the history of ontology.[44]

One consequence of these premises is that many positions and opinions fit within postmodernity. There is an enormous pluralism, which has led people to say that "everything goes" in this school of thought.[45] Reacting to positions seen as dogmatic and

---

42. "Modernity," says G. Vattimo, "ceases to exist when, for multiple reasons, the possibility of continuing to talk about history as a unitary entity disappears." See "Posmodernidad ¿una sociedad transparente?" in *En torno a la posmodernidad* (Barcelona: Anthropos, 1990) 10.

43. "Posmodernidad y fin de la historia," in *Etica de la interpretación* (Barcelona: Paidós ibérico, 1991) 28. Metaphysics is linked to the violence that I mentioned before. "The roots of metaphysical violence are ultimately in the authoritarian relationship metaphysics establishes between founding and founded." See G. Vattimo, "Ontología dell'attualità," *Filosofia '87* (Rome: Bari, Laterza, 1988) 201.

44. Cited in T. Oñate, "Introducción," in G. Vattimo, *La sociedad transparente* (Barcelona: Paidos, 1990) 38. I have taken the title of this section from this last author.

45. See Agnes Heller "Los movimientos culturales," in F. Viviescas and F. Giraldo, eds., *Colombia: el despertar de la modernidad* (Bogota: Foro nacional de Colombia, 1991).

totalitarian, these thinkers arrive at a cultural relativism tinged with a certain skepticism about the possibilities that a human being has for knowing. This skepticism has repercussions both in the field of ethics[46] and in that of politics.[47]

Without a doubt, the postmodern critique has highlighted the weaknesses and even the contradictions of modernity. Nevertheless, it should be remembered that modern thought always cultivated self-criticism. More than one of its representatives (F. Hegel is, in a way, one of them) expressed dissatisfaction with the effects of the Enlightenment. But now the critique is much more radical; moreover, it has gone beyond intellectual circles. As a stance toward life, it reaches diverse social sectors, some of which play a very active role in the cultural sphere and in the sphere of communications in contemporary society.[48]

The Fragmentation of Human Knowledge

There is something healthy, no doubt, in the reaction against totalizing visions of history that are part of the great narratives. These

---

46. Vattimo says, "The only global vision of reality that can seem plausible to us is a vision that takes the experience of fragmentation very seriously. . . . We shall only be able to reconstruct an ethic by beginning with an awareness of the impossibility of an ethics based on principles that are afterwards brought to realization as the application of a universal principle. Our ethic is the dissolution of universality." Interview in *Revista de Occidente* 104 (1990) 127.

47. Weak thought is "an effort to find a possibility of emancipation which is not linked to the rigidities of the revolutionary tradition, of dialectical politics." It is the possibility of "social transformation from within late-modern capitalism, in accord with the idea of those liberation movements which are internal to capitalist society and which do not imply as a condition for realization the seizing of power in the classical Leninist sense." See Vattimo, ibid., 126 and 123. This is one of the reasons why J. Habermas accuses postmodern thought of being a neoconservative movement in its politics. The German philosopher thinks that modernity is instead an "unfinished project."

48. See J. M. Mardones, *Postmodernidad y cristianismo* (Santander: Sal Terrae, 1988); and Scott Lash, *Sociology of Postmodernism* (London and New York: Routledge, 1990).

approaches involve an authoritarianism which has been carefully noted by postmodern thinkers. The poor have often seen themselves manipulated by projects that purport to be global but do not take persons and their daily lives into consideration and, while intensely focusing on the future, forget the present. But postmodern thought is not limited to this insight; it erodes all meaning from history, and this has an effect on the meaning assigned to each human existence. Furthermore, it identifies Hegel's philosophy of history with the Judeo-Christian concept of history and includes both in what it rejects.[49]

It is appropriate to recognize that the postmodern critique helps prevent us from falling into rigid and starchy models for interpreting the course of history. This has sometimes happened within the theological world. However, having said this, we must also recall that in a Christian perspective history has its center in the coming of the Son, in the Incarnation, which does not mean that human history advances ineluctably, following channels charted and controlled by a guiding concept made of iron. As the center of history, Jesus Christ is also the Way (cf. John 14:6) to the Father, a path that gives meaning to human existence and to the existence to which we are all called. This vocation gives the present—today—its full density, as I recalled in the introductory pages of this essay.

Postmodern knowledge rejects the grand narratives and values the small ones. In this way it helps us be more alert and sensitive to what is local and different (one of its main themes).[50] In a world that pays more and more attention to cultural diversity and to minorities (not without contradicting some of its other characteristics), this has important consequences. In the context of Latin America and the Caribbean, where indigenous minorities, the black population, and women seek to affirm their values and claim their rights,

---

49. It is appropriate to note, in view of this text, that although the influence of Christianity on Hegelian thought is incontrovertible, this does not lead to an identity between the two.

50. See G. Vattimo, *Le aventure della differenza* (Milan: Garzanti, 1980).

this feature of postmodernity can prove particularly fruitful and can be a corrective to a certain Western imperialism.

But we cannot dodge the fact that this sensitivity is linked to the intensification of individualism already present in modernity. The negation of the meaning of history increases individualism and reinforces the narcissism of contemporary society.[51] In this regard people have even talked about a second individualistic revolution.[52] We should take care that the critique of modernity's project does not conceal a desire to take refuge in individualism and indifference to others, which gives rise to a society closed in on itself.[53] This is clearly different from the challenge that liberation theology has been putting to modern thought for a long time.

On the other hand, contrary to what the modern outlook held, religion has not only not disappeared or been reduced to the private sphere but rather it shows a new vitality. The postmodern attitude can contribute to respecting mystery and thereby fostering what some consider the emergence of a new religious era.[54] There are many examples in the world of today. We must observe, nonetheless, that many times it is a matter of a vague and incoherent religiosity, bearing a generic belief about God or about an indeterminate divinity, mistrustful of firm convictions and antagonistic to the

---

51. See Christopher Lasch, *The Culture of Narcissism: American Life in an Age of Diminishing Expectations* (New York and London: Norton, 1991).

52. See A. Jiménez, "A vueltas con la postmodernidad," *Proyección* 155 (1989) 304. The author refers to G. Lipovetsky.

53. Helmut Peukert notes that the hermeneutic of difference about which postmodernists speak runs the risk of "thinking only about what is distinct in one's own thought instead of perceiving the distinct thought of others." See "Crítica filosófica de la modernidad," *Concilium* 244 (1992) 46.

54. "Both modernity with its values and counter-values and postmodernity as a space open to transcendence present serious challenges to the evangelization of culture." See CELAM, "Documento de Santo Domingo" (1992) no. 252. See also the rather critical reflections of J. Derrida and G. Vattimo in *La religión* (Madrid: PPC, 1996). To this we should add the new considerations offered by G. Vattimo in *Credere di credere* (Milan: Garzanti, 1996).

behaviors that these might lead to. But it is a fact of the present moment, and it will be necessary to take account of it from the perspective of faith.

The points recalled here, and certainly others, converge in an indifferent stance toward the possibilities of changing situations that, in the light of ethics, are seen as unjust and inhuman. The frustration produced by unfulfilled projects has resulted in a lack of interest in the fate confronted by the weakest members of society. We live in an era whose spirit is not very militant or committed. Within a neoliberal and postmodern framework, rooted in an aggressive individualism, solidarity seems ineffective and a remnant from the past.

If we add to this a skepticism that makes people think that all opinions are equal and that everyone has his or her own truth, as is often said, then everything goes. The reaction against all-encompassing visions, despite the healthy aspects that it does have, leads to the blotting out from the horizon of any utopia or project that is somewhat different from what presently exists. It goes without saying that the first victims of these views are the poor and marginalized for whom there seems to be very little room in the world that is being forged. It is always easy to criticize utopias from an unchanging *topos* in which people are satisfied.

However, as I've already indicated, being vigilant in the face of the effects of the present moment and knowing how to discern within this moment should not make us forget the values that are also found in this mentality. In this complex and sometimes even contradictory situation, we must bear witness to the reign of God, to solidarity with the poor, and to the liberation of those who see their most basic rights violated. Reflection on faith—theology—is summoned to be a hermeneutic of hope in our time: hope in the God of life, which is one of the main themes of the reflection that I have carried forward in these years.

Proclaiming the Reign

The observations made up to this point situate, and allow me to be concise in the presentation of, some aspects that need to be deepened theologically in the future. These are not completely new points; they belong to the Christian message that believers know and in which they recognize themselves as followers of Jesus and as church. The novelty lies in how they are tackled, in the challenges to which we seek to respond, in the previously unknown dimensions that familiar truths will disclose, and in the paths we take to express them.

This is also true for the proclamation of the gospel in which theological reflection is located and nourished. In this sense a new evangelization has been talked about.[55] John Paul II presented it like this: "new in its zeal, in its methods, in its expression."[56] On various occasions the pope energetically took up the subject again, and the Santo Domingo conference made it one of its central themes.

The perspective of new evangelization reappears as the "background" in the preparation for the third millennium (see TMA 21). For this purpose we must go deeper into "the conciliar vision" (ibid.) since the preparation for the Jubilee of the third millennium began with the Second Vatican Council. John Paul II spoke significantly of it as "a council similar to previous ones, although very different; a council centered on the mystery of Christ and of his church, and at the same time open to the world" (ibid., 18). "At the same time" means we are talking about two inseparable aspects. The salvific content of the mystery of Christ and his church must be communicated with an attitude of openness to the world. In this framework, I will take up some matters connected to certain paths with an eye toward this communication and toward the theological reflection that it implies.

---

55. The expression is found in the preparatory document for Medellín and in the "Message to the Peoples of Latin America" of that conference.

56. Address to CELAM in Port-au-Prince, Haiti, March 9, 1983.

Freed for Freedom

First, it is appropriate to make a few brief observations about the relationship between liberation and freedom, a core question for the theology of liberation.[57]

BETWEEN FREEDOM FROM AND FREEDOM FOR

The starting point is found in an important text of Paul in the letter to the Galatians which is focused on the theme of the Christian's freedom. "To be free [literally: for freedom] Christ freed us," says Paul (5:1). This is a liberation from sin, insofar as this signifies a selfish turning in on oneself; to sin is to refuse to love God and others. But for Paul it is also a liberation from the Law and from the forces of death (see Romans 8:2). In the Bible, sin, the breaking of friendship with God and with others, is the ultimate cause of injustice and oppression among human beings; it likewise causes all absence of personal freedom.[58] It is the ultimate cause because there are certainly other causes located at the level of economic and social structures as well as at the level of personal dimensions. Therefore no transformation of these structures and aspects is sufficient, no matter how radical it is. Only Christ's gratuitous and salvific love can go to the root of our very selves and make a true love spring up.

Nevertheless, Paul does not stop at saying that Christ freed us; he also asserts that he did it so that we might be free. According to a classical distinction, we must consider both freedom *from* and freedom *for*. The first points to sin, to selfishness, to oppression, to

---

57. For this section I take up what I have said in G. Gutiérrez, *Teología de la liberación: Perspectivas* (Lima: CEP, 1971, 1988 [2nd ed.]) 57-58 and 112-13, respectively; and in *Beber en su propio pozo* (Lima: CEP, 1986) 140-41; ET: *Theology of Liberation* (Maryknoll, NY: Orbis Books, 1971, 1988 [2nd ed.]) and *We Drink from Our Own Wells* (Maryknoll, NY: Orbis Books, 1984, 2003).

58. This is why I speak of three dimensions of integral liberation which are neither confused nor juxtaposed: social liberation, personal liberation, and soteriological liberation—that is, the liberation from sin and the entrance into communion with God and with others.

injustice, to privation, which are all conditions that demand libera-tion. The second points to the reason for this freedom: love, com-munion; this is the final stage of liberation. Freedom for gives free-dom from its deepest meaning. If we appeal to what is said in the same letter to the Galatians (5:13), we could say that the expression "free for love" synthesizes the Pauline position. Unless it reflects on freedom, a theology of liberation is left truncated.

Freedom is a central element of the Christian message. The accent on liberation should not make us forget this. It is important to establish a fruitful relationship between liberation and freedom. This becomes even more urgent in the face of certain questions today. They also lead us to underline the scope of another essential aspect of faith, closely linked to the theme of freedom. I am refer-ring to the link that Scripture introduces between truth and free-dom. "The truth will make you free," declares a famous text from John's Gospel (8:32). The truth is Christ himself who frees us and calls us to freedom (see Galatians 5:13). All human beings have a right to have this truth communicated to them, a proclamation that must not only respect freedom but must also establish freedom as such. On the other hand, this freedom cannot remain enclosed in an individual or solitary sphere. It finds its true meaning when it opens people to relationship with God and to the service of others with a special emphasis on the poorest and most deprived.[59]

The church's evangelizing work must make people truly free. Free to love. In accordance with this aim, theological reflection must be critical of any line of thought that renounces the search for truth and must take paths that allow us to go deeper into the gift of truth that makes us free.

His Reign and His Justice

At the heart of the Sermon on the Mount there is a verse that in a certain way sums up the whole: "Seek first *his* reign and *his* justice, and all other things will be given to you as well" (Matthew 6:33).

---

59. John Paul II devotes his encyclical *Veritatis splendor* to these themes.

The subject of the two possessive pronouns in the first clause is found in the previous verse: it is the "heavenly Father."

This search gives the Christian life its raison d'être. Thus, in a precise way and with a scope that must be taken into account, Matthew gives us the very heart of the entire Bible: everything comes from God. God is the Holy One, the totally Other, the One whose "designs are unfathomable and [whose] ways are inscrutable ... because from him and for him are all things" (Romans 11:33, 35). He is the source of life and love (Exodus 3:14; 1 John 4:16), a God who is far and near at the same time, who calls us to friendship with him, the foundation of the friendship that ought to exist among human beings. The holy God is also the incarnate God; embracing his love in our lives ought to be translated into life-giving acts toward others.

In our face-to-face meeting with God (1 Corinthians 13:12) human existence reaches its fullness. This is the hope and the experience of the mystics, the union with God of which they often speak. "My eyes have seen you," Job proclaims (42:5) when he grasps the fact that the gratuitous love of God, without limits or restrictions, is the foundation of the world and not his narrow concept of a kind of justice in which "you give me, and I give you." Having arrived at the end of the road, John of the Cross says poetically, "I remained, lost in oblivion, my face reclined on the Beloved ... among the lilies."[60] This was also expressed in a very beautiful way by Luis Espinal, a priest assassinated in Bolivia because of his commitment to the poor: "Lord of night and emptiness, we would like to know how to curl up in your intangible lap, confidently, with the security of children."[61] Mystical experience has always found in poetry the most appropriate language for expressing the mystery of love.

There is nothing more opposed to the search for God, his reign, and his justice than the service (in the strong sense of the term: cult) of an idol made by human hands. Idolatry, according to the Bible,

---

60. "Súbida del Monte Carmelo," in *Vida y obras de San Juan de la Cruz* (Madrid: BAC, 1950) 558.

61. *Oraciones a quemarropa* (Lima: CEP, 1982) 2.

means handing one's life over to and putting one's trust in something or someone other than God. This constitutes a permanent risk for the Christian. As I recalled above, in the neoliberal context of today, the market and profit are the object of idolatrous worship. For this reason, John Paul II spoke of the "idolatry of the market" (CA 40). This is the contemporary form of worshiping mammon. And then the idolatry of power, ignoring all human rights, is added to that of money. Victims are offered to these idols; this is why the biblical prophets always link idolatry and murder. Those who are excluded from the present international economic order are counted among the victims.

But we must go further still, even if this makes some people uncomfortable.[62] The idolatrous aspects of worshiping money and the will to power are, unfortunately, clear and massive in our time and disgust the human and Christian conscience. However, an idolatrous stance can also enter by the back door of our commitment to the liberation of the poor, regardless of how well inspired or motivated by Christian faith this may be. To assert this may seem strange at first sight, but we must see things as they are without mincing words or trying to sidestep reality.

It is possible, for example, to make justice into something close to an idol if we turn it into an absolute and do not know how to place it in a context that allows it to display its complete meaning, namely, gratuitous love. If there is no daily friendship with the poor and an appreciation of the diversity of their desires and needs as human beings, we can transform the search for justice into a pretext. Though it seems cruel to say this, experience teaches it. We can even turn our commitment to the poor into a justification for mistreating them, claiming that we know better than they do what they want and need.

---

62. In the following paragraphs I take up again some points that I presented in "Relectura de San Juan de la Cruz desde América Latina," found in *Actas del Congreso Internacional San Juanista,* vol. 3 (Junta de Castilla y León, 1993) 325-35; and in G. Gutiérrez, *Densidad del presente* (Lima: CEP–IBC, 1996).

We can also turn the poor themselves into a kind of idol. This happens when we idealize them, seeing them as simply good, generous, and deeply religious, believing that everything that comes from them is true and in a certain sense sacred. These qualities of the poor then become the principal reason for our solidarity with them. And we forget that the poor are human beings pierced by both grace and sin, as St. Augustine would say. There is no doubt that we find enormous amounts of generosity and selflessness in them, but to conclude that this is true in every case is to fail to recognize the complexity and the ambiguity of persons. The idealization of the poor, which is what those who are not poor (and sometimes, though more rarely, the poor themselves) do, does not lead to liberation. In addition, and above all, we must remember that for Christians the ultimate reason for their commitment to the poor is not found in their moral or religious qualities, although these exist, but rather in God's goodness, which ought to inspire our own conduct.

On the other hand, and in an even subtler way, my own theology and, of course, the theology of liberation, which we have tried to elaborate in Latin America beginning with the sufferings and hopes of the poor, can likewise become a kind of idol. This happens when in practice it becomes more important than the faith that illuminates it or the reality it seeks to express. This is the risk we run in any intellectual work that we hold on to more than we should. Those whose names are attached to theological texts must not forget that they are not the real witnesses of the Latin American church, which seeks to demonstrate its faith in the God of the Bible through its solidarity with the poor. Or not necessarily, to be more exact. Instead, the true witnesses are those who often anonymously, and at the risk of their own lives, live out their pastoral and social commitment in their everyday existence. They are anonymous to the media and to the world at large, but not to God.

For all these reasons, testimonies such as those of John of the Cross and so many others from the church's mystical tradition are so important for our theological reflection. With the scalpel of their experience and their poetry, they help us eliminate everything that is in some way infected with idolatry and self-absorption, every-thing that makes us put what is secondary in the forefront of our search and keeps us from seeing and feeling that only God is God.

In every situation it is essential for Christians to keep the pri-macy of God in their lives. Spirituality—that is, the following of Jesus—is thus not only a pertinent concern in theology; it is its real foundation. This becomes more urgent in a way when Christians are immersed in what the popes call "the noble struggle for justice." We are talking about God's justice, in its double biblical sense of justice among human beings and holiness. It is tightly linked to God's reign of life and love, as shown by the Matthean text cited above.

For this reason, and for the ones just given, the theme of spiritu-ality has been central in liberation theology from the beginning, or in much of it at least. It is a reflection on a faith that is located in the tension between mysticism and historical commitment. I recalled above that the preferential option for the poor to which this theol-ogy is tied is a theocentric option. As a genuine decision to stand with the real poor of the world today, its foundation is in the gratu-ity of God's love, the ultimate reason for the preference. The mysti-cal foundation is essential for the proclamation of God's reign and that reign's requirements of justice.[63]

This line of spiritual deepening is one of the great tasks facing evangelization and theological reflection in our time. What ought to be the very backbone of Christian existence is at stake here: the consciousness of God and the presence of God's love in our lives. It's not a matter of balancing our commitment in history by appealing

---

63. For these reasons, those who think (and write) that liberation theology got involved in the field of spirituality and mysticism over the years because of debates provoked by positions it had taken do not know the sources or the trajectory of this reflection on faith. They also forget that Christian spiritu-ality does not move in some ethereal sphere but rather always shows—and must show—a connection to daily life and solidarity with others, especially the weakest of society. The spiritual experiences that people have had in Latin America, and which reach the point of surrendering their lives, move in this direction.

to spiritual dimensions but rather of deepening that commitment and giving it its full meaning and radicality. For this purpose, it is important to practice theology as wisdom—and critical to restore this if necessary. Theology should be like savoring something, a delicious knowledge of the Word of God, a wisdom with a flavor aimed at enriching the daily life of the believer and of the entire Christian community. Furthermore, this allows us to open ourselves to other forms of knowing Christian truths, even while appreciating the role that reason plays in theological reflection. Symbolic language, for example, is particularly fruitful in this regard.

The Question of the Other

In the opinion of Carlos Fuentes, the greatest problem of the twenty-first century will be the problem of the other. This is an old concern in the framework of liberation theology, which sees the poor person as "the other" of a society more and more satisfied with itself. In any case, it is undeniable that we are living through a moment of contracting distances on the planet (global village) and, at the same time, of expanding awareness of the diversity of peoples, cultures, genders, ethnic groups, and religions. These are not contradictory movements, as one might imagine. Indeed, we can say that in a certain way they mutually reinforce each other, although at times they openly confront each other and produce dangerous whirlwinds.

IDENTITY AND DIALOGUE

In Latin America ancient indigenous peoples have made their voice of protest heard for humiliations suffered over centuries. But they have also raised their voices to enrich others with the wealth of their cultures, their love for the earth, source of life, their experience of respect for the natural world and its communal significance, the depth of their religious values, and the value of their theological reflection.[64] Taking account of the nuances appropriate to each case,

64. See the results of two conferences published in *Teología India I* (México) (Mexico City: Cenami; Quito: Abya Yala, 1991); and *Teología*

we can say that something similar has happened with the black population of Latin America,[65] and with the new presence of women, especially those who belong to the marginalized and oppressed sectors.[66] This has led to a fruitful dialogue among different theological points of view.[67]

It is important to make distinctions at the heart of these human groups, for they are not uniform aggregations. It is likewise necessary to keep in mind the growing affirmation of the values of the poor that are the result of the crosses—age-old and also very recent—common on our continent of "all races," as José María Arguedas used to say of Peru. I am thinking not only of the racial aspect but also the cultural, and culture is in a permanent state of development. Indeed, culture does not belong to the past but rather is a continuous creation, both faithful to and breaking with a particular tradition. This gives it its capacity to resist attitudes and ideas

---

India II (Panamá)(Quito: Abya-Yala, 1994). In the latter book, see E. López, "Tendencias de la teología india hoy," 5-26.

65. See the collective work *Cultura negra y teología* (San José, Costa Rica: DEI, 1986); and Antonio Aparecido da Silva, "Jesus Cristo luz e libertador do povo afro-americano. Ensaio de cristología experencial," in *Revista ecclesiástica brasileira* (September 1996) 636-63.

66. See three collective works: Maria Clara Bingemer et al., *El rostro femenino de la teología* (San José, Costa Rica: DEI, 1986; ET, Elsa Tamez, ed., *Through Her Eyes: Women's Theology from Latin America* [Maryknoll, NY: Orbis Books, 1989]); María Pilar Aquino, ed., *Aportes para una teología desde la mujer* (Madrid: Biblia y Fe, 1988); and Elsa Tamez, ed., *Las mujeres toman la palabra* (San José, Costa Rica: DEI, 1989). See also Ada María Isasi-Díaz and Yolanda Tarango, *Hispanic Women: Prophetic Voice in the Church* (San Francisco: Harper & Row, 1988); Adelaida Sueiro, "La mujer, un rostro del pobre en el Perú," *Páginas* 134 (1995) 60-76; and Barbara Pataro Bucker, *O femenino da igreja e o conflito* (Petropolis: Vozes, 1995).

67. See G. Gutiérrez, "Reflections from a Latin American Perspective: Finding Our Way to Talk about God," in Virginia Fabella and Sergio Torres, eds., *Irruption of the Third World* (Maryknoll, NY: Orbis Books, 1983) 222-34; and Diego Irarrázaval, "Nuevas rutas de la teología latinoamericana," *Revista latinoamericana de teología* 38 (1996) 183-97.

that dilute its identity. The past and present of the people—of the peoples—of our continent are full of examples of this.

On the other hand, as I have already pointed out, the postmodern frame of mind, which reaches different social strata in waves and with its ambiguities, is inclined to appreciate the local and the unique. We cannot forget, however, that this is done with an obvious skepticism that relativizes any possibility of asserting universal truths.

To proclaim the gospel is to initiate a salvific dialogue. It presupposes respect for the other and his or her particularities.[68] It does not try to impose itself but rather to serve and persuade.[69] What we call "inculturation of faith" today should point to this; it doubtless belongs to an old experience of the church. It refers to a double movement: Christian faith must constantly take flesh in new cultural values, and we can say as well that cultures must take on the gospel message.

Nevertheless, it is important to note that dialogue implies interlocutors who are aware of their own identity. Christian faith and theology cannot forswear their sources or their personality in order to enter into contact with other points of view. To have firm convictions is not an obstacle to dialogue but rather it is a requirement. To accept the truth of Jesus Christ in our lives, not by our own effort but by the grace of God, not only does not invalidate our intercourse with people of other perspectives but rather gives it its genuine significance. While some seem to be living with the loss of frames of reference, it is germane to recall that identity, a humble and open identity, is an essential component of a spirituality.

---

68. In 1995 John Paul II recalled the need to have a sense of the other and not to fear "difference." See his address to the 50th General Assembly of the United Nations (October 10, 1995).

69. In his eloquent address to the second conciliar session, Paul VI said that "the world should know this: the church looks upon it ... with the sincere intention not of conquering it but rather of serving it; not of condemning it but rather of comforting and saving it" (September 29, 1963). This is a perspective that has lost none of its relevance today.

What I have just said may seem obvious. But I'm thinking of that tendency found today in many people and in many Christians who believe that there can be no authentic dialogue if, in one way or another, we do not renounce our convictions and our understanding of the truth. This attitude comes from the fear—unfortunately illustrated by many painful historical examples—of a Christian point of view being imposed by force. The danger is real, and it is right to acknowledge it. But the proposed solution leads nowhere. Besides, contrary to what is sometimes thought, it shows a lack of respect for those who receive our communication of the gospel. We ought to express our convictions clearly to them, just as we show them our respect for theirs.

Skepticism, relativism, and "weak thought" do not lead to an adequate language for a dialogue that is truly respectful and profitable. The great challenge is to know how to carry it out without hiding or diluting the truths, and their consequences, in which we believe. This is required by faith and by honesty.[70] But, once again, as I've already said, we must have a great capacity for listening and for being open to what the Lord can say to us from other human, cultural, and religious perspectives. We could say, in what is only an apparent paradox, that the firmer our convictions and the more transparent our Christian identity, the greater our capacity to hear others.

The preferential option for the poor and the excluded, the heart of the biblical message, is today an important element of Christian and ecclesial identity. Its reference to the heavenly Father who gives

---

70. In our time it is possible to see the importance of a point that needs clarification in the dialogue with the great religions of humanity and also in some cases—limited, it is true, but notable—in Latin America. I'm referring to Jesus Christ, the Son of God made man, one of us in history, a Jew, son of Mary, belonging to a particular people. The historicity of Jesus can create problems for religious perspectives that find it hard to accept elements they understand as coming from outside their cultural traditions. Nevertheless, the historical character of the Incarnation is a central element of Christian faith. In addition, and for all cases, we'll need to go deeper into what categories within and outside of our own history signify intellectually.

us his reign and his justice is basic; its christological foundation is clear and obvious.[71] It carries the seal of the love and freedom brought to us by the Holy Spirit. This option constitutes an intrinsic element of ecclesial identity. It contributes in this way, beginning with a feature proper to the Christian message, to opening a dialogue with other perspectives in the bosom of the ecclesial community and beyond it. To deepen our thinking about a humble but firm Christian and ecclesial identity, and to carry forward a fruitful evangelization in this way, is one of the demanding tasks of theology today in the face of the many uncertainties, questions, and also possibilities of the contemporary world. This is certainly also the case for liberation theology.

AN ETHIC OF SOLIDARITY

The indigenous peoples of Latin America have practiced solidarity and reciprocity for centuries. I am thinking, for example, of the collective (or reciprocal) work that members of the same community offer to one another.[72] There is much to be learned from this experience, which belongs not only to the past but rather is still alive in our own time.

Furthermore, in recent times the term "solidarity" and reflection on it have been common themes in Latin America. For Christians solidarity expresses an efficacious love for all and in particular for the most vulnerable of society. It's not a matter of personal acts alone; solidarity is required of the entire social aggregation and signifies a commitment of the entire church.

---

71. This perspective has been present from the very beginning of the recent prehistory of the expression "preferential option for the poor." See the complete text of Cardinal Giacomo Lercaro's remarks, which had to be abbreviated in his presentation during the first conciliar session on December 6, 1962 (Giacomo Lercaro, *Per la forza dello Spirito: Discorsi conciliari* [Bologna: Edizioni Dehoniane, 1984] 113-22).

72. In the Andean world we call it *mink'a*. See E. Meyer, "Las reglas del juego en la reciprocidad andina," in G. Alberti and E. Meyer, eds., *Reciprocidad e intercambio en los Andes peruanos* (Lima: IEP, 1974) 37-65.

Today the subject of solidarity has assumed international proportions. And the more that powerful schools of thought linked to neoliberalism and postmodernity discredit and reject solidary behavior in the name of radical individualism, the more urgent the subject becomes. These ways of thinking consider solidarity archaic, inefficacious, and (though this seems strange to me) even counterproductive in the development of peoples, especially for their least powerful members. This is the basis for their appreciation of egoism, a word they are not afraid to use, which they consider a stimulus for economic activity and for the accumulation of wealth, which (according to them) does not affect the poor at all. On the other hand, although this element converges with the previous one, the sector of humanity fascinated by new forms of knowledge tends to close in on itself and break off solidarity with those with whom it communicates less and less.[73]

John Paul II, beginning with his letter on human work, issued repeated calls for solidarity among workers themselves, among the poor in general, and of course among rich and poor countries. In his apostolic letter about the third millennium, he begins with Luke 4:16-20 and highlights the meaning of the biblical theme of the Jubilee for the world situation precisely as an expression of solidarity because it is "a time dedicated in a special way to God" (TMA 11).

In the Lucan text, based on Isaiah as we know, the key theme is freedom. Three of its verses allude to freedom (liberation of captives; sight for the blind, that is, for prisoners, according to the Hebrew text of the prophet; and freedom for the oppressed). Freedom from all types of death (sin, oppression) is thus linked to the equality that we must begin to reestablish in a year of grace which is nothing other than a time of solidarity. All of this constitutes the subject matter of the Good News that must be proclaimed to the poor. Taking his cue from this passage, John Paul II beseeches us to proclaim, once again, with words and deeds, Jesus' messianic message.

---

73. See the observations of E. Arens in this regard in "Neoliberalismo y valores cristianos," *Páginas* 137 (1996) 47-59.

Two consequences are of particular interest for our commitment and our theological reflection. The first concerns the updating and deepening of a theme of biblical and patristic antecedents: the universal purpose of the goods of the earth. Today more than ever it is appropriate to recall that God has given the entire human race what is needed for its livelihood. The goods of this world do not belong exclusively to certain persons or social groups, no matter what their position in society or their level of knowledge may be. They belong to all. Only within this framework can we accept the private appropriation of what is required for existence and of what is desirable for a better social order.

This matter has been present from the very beginning of the church's modern-day social teaching (cf. Leo XIII), but has acquired more and more weight and new scope.[74] In the face of an economic order presented as the natural order, which regulates itself—controlled by the famous "invisible hand"—for the benefit of all, which makes profit and consumption an unconditional motor of economic activity, which pillages the earth and is in search of places to deposit industrial waste, the assertion of the universal purpose of the goods of this world must be further examined and deepened.

A consideration of this will show, despite what some may think or refute, that we are not talking about an illusory or romantic vision of social existence. It is rather a focus called on to mobilize personal energies because of faith in the God of life, of human solidarity, and also (it's important to accept this) for historical efficacy.[75] We have clear examples of this resolve today. This is a utopian perspective, if you wish, but in the realistic meaning of the term, which rejects an inhuman situation and proposes relationships of justice and

---

74. See John Paul II, CA 30-87; and TMA 13 and 51.

75. See the important experiences and reflections about a popular solidary economy presented by L. Razeto in *Economía popular de solidaridad* (Santiago: Area pastoral social de la conferencia episcopal de Chile, 1986); and in *Crítica de la economía, mercado democrático y crecimiento* (Santiago: Programa de economía del trabajo, 1994).

cooperation among persons.[76] Whether the term "utopia" is used or not, the important thing is not to resign ourselves to suffering, hunger, and lack of freedom for so many, and the absence of democratic transparency in many nations. It is also essential to be convinced that humanity's real advances allow us to glimpse the possibility of forging a situation different from the present one.

The second consequence that I want to underline is the one that refers to the stifling problem of the foreign debt. It's clear that poor countries cannot pay it except at the cost of the life and pain of huge swaths of their population. Thus, this is above all an ethical question. In some way every important economic question that affects the lives of people is ethical, but with the question of the debt we stand before something so obvious that it becomes monstrous to claim that it is limited to a technical question. There is no doubt that responsibility must be shared in this. Although it's true that the crisis of the 1970s pressed international agencies, banks, and countries to invest their money in poor nations, we cannot hide the part played by political leaders and those who managed the economy of developing peoples.

But it is obvious that paying the debt would leave—has already left—millions of poor people without a place to sleep. Many reasons can be adduced for cancelling the debt.[77] But the most decisive

---

76. See the description of and reflection on valuable experiences along these lines presented by Carmen Lora in *Creciendo en dignidad: Movimiento de comedores autogestionarios* (Lima: IBC–CEP, 1996).

77. Of the historical kind, for example, given the asymmetrical economic relations, so to speak, between the rich countries and those that were their colonies for centuries. Some decades ago John Maynard Keynes made a disturbing calculation in all seriousness. According to the English economist, if the treasure stolen by the pirate Drake from Spain at the end of the sixteenth century (this is how Keynes refers to one part, quite small in the final analysis, of the gold coming from what today we call Latin America and the Caribbean) had accumulated compound interest at the modest rate of 3.25%, by 1930 the resulting amount would represent the sum total of England's foreign investments (see "Economic Possibilities for Our Grandchildren," in Keynes, *Collected Writings*, IX. 323-24).

is ethical—the life and death of so many persons. The church's mag-isterium has spoken clearly in this regard.[78] Present simultaneously in both rich countries and in poor nations, the church has an impor-tant role in this matter.

The symbolic date (which the great dates of history always are) of the year 2000 was lifted up by the Jubilee proposed in TMA.[79] The biblical significance of joy at the love of the Lord, of the proc-lamation of freedom, of the reestablishment of equality and justice, and of the proclamation of the Good News to the poor is a call to solidarity and to reflection. It is also a call to creativity so that it does not remain a frivolous celebration of the turn of a millennium. The fate of the poor and the excluded, and what their fate implies in relation to our fidelity to the God of Jesus Christ, represents a demanding and fertile challenge for liberation theology and for theology in general.

The God of Life

In the final analysis, poverty, as I have earlier suggested, means death. It is physical death for many persons and cultural death due to contempt for so many others.[80] An awareness of this situation led, a few decades ago, to the rise of the theme of life, gift of the God of our faith. The early onset of Christians being assassinated for their witness turned our concern into something even more

---

78. See John Paul II, CA 35 and TMA 51 (which speaks of "total con-demnation"); Pontifical Commission on Justice and Peace, "At the Service of the Human Community: An Ethical Approach to the International Debt" (1986); and CELAM, Santo Domingo document, nos. 197-98.

79. For a biblical study of the theme of jubilee in relation to Jesus' mes-sage, see Sharon Ringe, *Jesus, Liberation, and the Biblical Jubilee: Images for Ethics and Christology* (Philadelphia: Fortress Press, 1985).

80. It is suggestive to see how the perspective of death and life is taken into account in the field of economics. By the notable scholar Amartya Sen, see "La vida y la muerte como indicadores económicos," *Investigación y ciencia* (1993) 6-13.

urgent.[81] Reflection on the experience of persecution and martyrdom has given strength and scope to a theology of life, allowing us to see that the option for the poorest is precisely an option for life.

It is a decision, in the final analysis, for the God of life, for the "friend of life," as it says in the book of Wisdom (11:25). In these expressions we find a way of saying that faith and hope inspire the Christian's commitment. Experiencing violence and unjust death up close leaves no room for evasions or abstract considerations of Jesus' resurrection without which our faith would be in vain, as Paul puts it. The resurrection also makes us sensitive to the gift of life that we receive from God, a life that comprises spiritual and religious elements as well as those we usually call material and bodily.

On the other hand, the experience of these years has broadened our view of social solidarity, which must be aware of the importance of a respectful link with nature. The ecological issue does not affect only the industrial countries that cause greater destruction in the natural habitat of human beings. It concerns all of humanity, as many studies and numerous church documents have shown. We say—rightly—that the planet Earth is a great ship on which we are all passengers. Nevertheless, the same image can help us remember that some on this common vessel travel in first class while others travel third class. No one is excused, of course, from the task of preventing the destruction of life in our natural environment. But looking at things from the vantage point of poor countries, we must pay special attention to what affects the weakest members of humanity. And we must thus reaffirm our faith in the God of life, above all with the peoples who have always had a sacred sense of the earth.

This view can be inferred from corrections that the Bible introduces in advance to an abusive interpretation of "dominate the

---

81. John Paul II's comment that "at the end of the second millennium the Church has again become the Church of martyrs" is easily understood today in Latin America and the Caribbean. Especially when he adds, "*In our century the martyrs have returned*, often nameless" (TMA 37; emphasis in the original). But this affirmation is certainly valid for other regions of the world as well.

earth" (see Genesis) made by the modern West through what Habermas calls instrumental reason. We find such corrections, for example, in the book of Job, whose author affirms that it is not the human being but rather the gratuitous love of God that is the center and meaning of all created reality. A theology of creation and of life can breathe oxygen into a theology that is constructed with a concern for justice, a theology that thereby helps us broaden our horizon.[82] Here we certainly have a fruitful task for theological reflection on liberation.

Such a theology will make us more sensitive to the aesthetic dimensions of the process of integral liberation, and for this very reason it will try to take into consideration all aspects of the human being. The right to beauty is an expression, and in a certain sense an urgent one, of the right to life. The human being has needs but also desires, and in this the postmodernists are right. Our bodily dimension links us in a special way to the natural world and is the source of delight in the gift of life. But it is also a challenge: often famished and aching, the bodies of the poor also groan as they anxiously await "the revelation of the children of God," as Paul says in a beautiful and somewhat mysterious text (Romans 8:19).

One example of the commitment to life is the defense of human rights. During the 1970s the actions of Latin American and Caribbean dictatorships caused many people to do their utmost in this effort. This experience became a path that led to proposals for the democratic common life that was needed. Because of this, it was not limited to denouncing flagrant abuses of authority but rather early on pointed the finger at the political instability and social injustice that constitute the breeding ground for other kinds of violence.

It is appropriate to recall here John Paul II's remark about the "human environment" (after having dealt with the natural environ-

---

82. See J. Moltmann, *Zukunft der Schöpfung* (Munich: Kaiser Verlag, 1977); R. Coste, *Dieu et l'écologie* (Paris: Editions de l'Atelier, 1994); and, from a Latin American perspective, L. Boff, *Ecología: Grito da terra. Grito dos pobres* (São Paulo: Editora Atica, 1996); ET, *Cry of the Earth, Cry of the Poor* (Maryknoll, NY: Orbis Books, 1997).

ment), which leads him to speak about "human ecology" in relation to social structures (see CA 38-39).[83] With this we face a central—and novel—theme for life considered as a gift from God.

Theology has before it an important task if it wishes to go deeper into the faith in a God who is not a God of fear but rather, as Albert Camus said, "who laughs with us as we play sweltering games by the sea and in the sun." A God of life and happiness.

Conclusion

The present moment makes us see the urgency of something that might seem very elementary: giving meaning to human existence. Various factors mentioned throughout these pages come together to weaken or disperse reference points and make it hard for people today, perhaps especially young people, to see the why and the wherefore of their lives. Without this, among other things, the struggle for a more just social order and human solidarity loses steam and has no bite.

A key task in the proclamation of the gospel today is to contribute to giving life meaning. Perhaps in the early stages of theological work in Latin America, we took it for granted, just as we considered the inspiration of faith and the affirmation of the fundamental truths of the Christian message as givens. Whatever the case, it is certain that at present we must worry about the very foundations of the human condition and of the life of faith.

Once again, it seems to me that the commitment to the poor, as a choice centered on the gratuitous love of God, has an important word to say in this matter. It stands in what I described a few pages back as the tension between mysticism and solidarity in history.

---

83. In this human ecology we will have to consider the contamination that comes from the corruption seen at high levels of political and economic power. This is a genuine sickness, which, although also present in industrialized nations, is capable of bringing down poor countries' feeble efforts at development.

This is only a way, perhaps a somewhat abstract way, of repeating what the gospel says with complete simplicity: love for God and love for neighbor sum up the message of Jesus.

This is what really matters. I must confess that I am less concerned about the good or the survival of liberation theology than I am about the sufferings and hopes of the people to whom I belong, and especially about the communication of the experience and the message of salvation in Jesus Christ. The latter is the substance of our love and our faith. No matter how relevant a theology's function is, it is only one way of deepening love and faith. Theology is a hermeneutic of hope lived as a gift of the Lord. This, indeed, is what it's about: proclaiming hope to the world in the moment we are living through as church.

CHAPTER 6

The Common Future of the Church

GERHARD LUDWIG MÜLLER

Gustavo Gutiérrez's contributions to theology have clearly brought something into view for us in Europe: injustice in the world is a persistent factor that can be overcome only through the deliberate step of directing the attention of all people to Christ. The decisive questions that are significant to all human beings concerning their origin, their purpose, and the manner of their existence find their fulfillment and resolution in the deliberate step of acknowledging Christ as the Lord and the fulfillment of all human beings. With this realization, there is now a new stimulus for theology, even in Europe. The orientation to Jesus Christ, the savior and liberator of the whole human family, has become the appropriate emphasis of every theology.

However, have we adequately comprehended the living conditions in the countries of South America? Oppressive poverty daily takes the lives of thousands of children, elderly people, and those who are ill because the basic infrastructure for life-giving care is not available. Do we know the anxiety that people suffer who are imprisoned in their illnesses and oftentimes must accept the glimmering hope of death as the way out of their misery, while they are also aware that in Europe the medical infrastructure would rescue their lives by means of a small intervention?

Among the existential needs and dangers in Latin America, the deficient forms of education stand out as humiliating expressions of intentional oppression. An aspect of the intentional oppression of people in poverty can include the refusal both to recognize the grave causes of poverty and also to eliminate these causes. The successful formal education in wide parts of the First World generates a feeling of superiority in relation to the countries of the so-called Third World. Doesn't this attitude of superiority make secure the roots of intellectual as well as material exploitation?

Someone who has direct encounters with the people of South America notices that the people's joy and vitality of faith are tangible and evident. The often vibrant faith, which is communicated with love, stands out as one of the greatest riches of these men and women who are burdened by the daily cares of their own lives.

Through many personal encounters, this joyous and living faith itself has become a motivation and an inspiration for me. One is challenged to think about the essential conditions of human life and also to be responsible to God, the creator and fulfillment of all human beings. Daily suffering is the reality of which the people of South America speak when they pray the Lord's Prayer asking for their "daily bread" (Matthew 6:11). What moves their lips is not consumer-driven satisfaction but immense hunger.

In the economically and politically tense situations of the countries of Latin America, most people find their hope as well as their shelter and existential security in the church. Indeed, they tell their life stories in relation to the church. That their self-understanding exists as they confess the church's faith and that they live out this faith in relation to the trust that they have for the church and theology become either problems or insignificant themes for representatives of German theology and the ecclesiastical "establishment."

Is it not the case that the destructive and relentless criticism in Germany of the church comes from people who call themselves Christian? Could we not learn something in this regard from the Latin American people who entrust themselves to the church because they see in the church the illuminating point of reference for their lives? In contrast, many bourgeois, established theologians in Germany often obstruct the way forward. On the one hand, they demand a new beginning, a fundamental change in the church during the twenty-first century, and yet, on the other hand, they entangle themselves in a complexity of themes that surely hinders this fundamental change.

The church has wide appeal and credibility when it understands itself as God's sacrament in the world and for the world (*Lumen gentium* 1), God's sacrament that brings about the unbreakable bond of people with God and thus leads them to their proper destiny. The radical character of the church's proclamation is evident in its differentiation in relation to the world. The church exposes people's extreme this-worldliness, which ultimately robs them of their appropriate fundamental attitude as God's creatures. Out of their state as God's creatures, there can emerge their personalities and their dignity, which includes their inviolability and eternal value in relation to God. Instead of [theologians] persisting in ever-increasing demands, which become completely unimportant in light of the needs of the people in Latin America, it would be more productive for them to show the illuminating power of faith for the salvation of all people.

The position of the church in South America is indisputably great. The church's diligence and deliberateness in upholding the importance of the poorest people are the result of a truly applied and lived faith.

The responsibility is great. Many sects and pseudo-religious groups have access to the people. To offer assistance here is an important task, which European Christians could perform because South American communities, lacking financial means, are often helpless in relation to the financially powerful religious sects. In this regard, the church can serve the global growth of interconnectedness among people in which it attains unity on a higher level than is possible on the basis of purely natural associations.

My special gratitude extends to my friend Gustavo Gutiérrez. During the past decades, he has explained the coherence-establishing dimensions of the so-called theology of liberation, and he has produced comprehensive overviews of this theology in numerous texts. Even though the theology of liberation has often been contentiously discussed, this theological endeavor is nevertheless no closed chapter in the history of theology. Broadening our angle of perception, which is concentrated on Europe, Gustavo Gutiérrez clarifies for us what it means to be world church. With the theology of liberation, the Catholic Church is able to construct its internal plurality even more broadly. The theology of Latin America frees new, additional aspects of theology that are placed completely on the margins of the often-encrusted forms of theology in Europe.

The ecclesiological language of *communio*, in which the church is seen to be a world-encompassing community that exists beyond ethnic and national categories, is meant to lead the world-encompassing community of faithful people to a sense of their responsible solidarity. In the parable of the last judgment, Jesus taught: "Truly I tell you, just as you did it to one of the least of these who are members of my family, you did it to me" (Matthew 25:40). As Christians, we are not permitted to withdraw from this responsibility. We are not permitted to remain blind to the need and the poverty that our brothers and sisters in the faith in Jesus Christ must endure.

The Second Vatican Council acknowledged the worldwide responsibility of Christians in its Pastoral Constitution on the Church in the Modern World, *Gaudium et spes* 1, in the following words: "The joys and hopes, grief and anguish of the people of our time, especially of those who are poor or afflicted, are the joys and hopes, the grief and anguish of the followers of Christ as well." The council sees itself bound to the human family that is growing increasingly closer. The catholicity spoken of here in its original meaning as universal, encompassing everything, finds its decisive expression in the council's Dogmatic Constitution on the Church, *Lumen gentium* 1, when it speaks of the "present situation" which gives the church "greater urgency," "so that all people, who nowadays are drawn ever more closely together by social, technical, and cultural bonds, may achieve closer unity in Christ."

The one church of Jesus Christ goes beyond the divisions of national, ethnic, and political walls, and it leads people to their innermost unity with God and with one another (see once again *Lumen gentium* 2). The Bible describes Jesus Christ as our rescuer who brings us liberation and salvation. He liberates people from sin in its personal and its structural forms, from sin which is ultimately the cause of the breaking of friendships and ultimately the cause of every kind of injustice and oppression. Christ alone sets us free in truth and leads us to freedom which is given to us by God. On the basis of this freedom, we are called by God to help people because everyone who is poor and in need is our neighbor.

I intend this book to be both a contribution to overcoming indifference about the suffering and the needs of our brothers and sisters and also a contribution to the set of coordinates by which to arrive at the correct appraisal of the theology of liberation—the theology that directs our minds to Christ who, as our rescuer and savior, is the goal toward whom we irresistibly strive. Gustavo Gutiérrez has expressed this view in entirely simple, biblical terms: "Christian life exists in following Jesus Christ."

Following Christ means concrete action: "But those who do what is true come to the light, so that it may be clearly seen that their deeds have been done in God" (John 3:21). Thus the Lord gives us the witness to engage ourselves in an immediate manner for the people who are poor. Doing the truth brings us to stand with people who live in poverty.

—Translated by Robert A. Krieg

Index

Alfaro, Juan, 27
Arguedas, José María, 122

base communities, 15, 63
Berlin Wall, fall of, 22
Bernard of Clairvaux, 52
Blondel, Maurice, 27
Boff, Clodovis, on liberation
	theology, 57
Bonhoeffer, Dietrich, 26
	on church for others, 74

capitalism
	in Latin American context, 24
	and liberation theology, 23, 24,
		25, 68, 69
	and oppression, 67, 68
	savage, 94, 95
Catholic social teaching, 14, 60
Centesimus annus (John Paul II), 89,
	96, 118, 129, 132
Chenu, M. D., and spirituality, 50,
	51
Christ, as foundation of preferential
	option, 10
church
	as communio, 12, 30, 137
	in context of liberation theology,
		74-76
	European and Latin American,
		134-38
	as God's sacrament, 136

Latin American, 15, 16
	and listening to divergent
		opinions, 7
	as location of theology, 2, 7
	prophetic ministry of, 2
	responsibility of, for human
		society, 12, 13
	and role of theologian, 2, 3
	as sign of God's saving will, 12
	theology in service of, 7
	universal, 137, 138
	world, and work of Gutiérrez,
		136, 137
Committee of Santa Fe, secret
	document of, 23, 24
cross, and preferential option for the
	poor, 73
culture and faith
	in Europe, 28, 29
	in Latin America, 29

democracy, and human rights, 25
dependence theory, 77, 96, 97
dialogue, with the poor, 121-25
dignity, of human person, 6, 9, 18,
	20

economy
	dehumanization of, 48, 49
	and ethics, 97-101
environment, protection of, 130,
	131

ethics, and the economy, 97-101
evangelization
    inculturated, 9
    new, 8, 9, 31, 114
    and theology, 2-4, 7

faith
    contemporary challenges to, 33,
        34
    and liberation theology, 87
    and love, 62
    and theology, 2
Fides et ratio (John Paul II), 20
First Commandment, and poverty, x
foreign debt, 49, 95, 128, 129
free-market capitalism, 94, 95. *See
        also* neoliberal economic
        theory
freedom
    as central element of Christian
        message, 116
    and liberation, 115-21
freedom from, and freedom for, 115,
    116
Friedman, Milton, 25, 94
Fuentes, Carlos, and problem of the
    other, 121

Gaudium et spes
    and humanization, 75, 76
    poor, as personal subjects, viii, x,
        xi
    as source of liberation theology,
        14, 56
    and worldwide responsibility of
        Christians, 137
globalization
    of the economy, 93-113
    and poverty, 47-50
    and social justice, xiii

God
    as God of life, 129-32
    as only theme of theology, 3, 85
goods of the earth, universal purpose
        of, 127
grace and sin
    and idealization of the poor, 119
    liberation theology perspective
        on, 77, 78
    social character of, 69, 70, 77

Habermas, J., on postmodernity, 111
history, liberation theology's
        understanding of, 78, 79
horizontalism, and liberation
        theology, 14, 28
human being, dignity of, 6, 9, 18, 20
human promotion, 8, 9
human rights, defense of, 131

idolatry, 117, 118, 119
Iglesias, Enrique, 93
immanentizing, and liberation
        theology, 14
immigration, and the poor, 101
inculturation, 9
individualism, 36, 126
    and modernity, 112
"Instruction on the Ecclesial
        Vocation of the Theologian"
        (CDF), 2
integral development, 99
interreligious dialogue, 37, 38

Jesus, in context of liberation
        theology, 72, 73
John of the Cross, 117, 119
John Paul II
    call for solidarity by, 126
    and cancellation of debt, 49

and Catholic social teaching, 9, 14, 99
and class struggle, 5
and divergent opinions in the church, 7
and human environment, 131, 132
and idolatry of the market, 118
on liberation theology, 18; necessity of, 56
and new evangelization, 8, 9, 114
and preferential option for the poor, ix, xiii, 7, 41, 89
and religious pluralism, 37
and social justice, xiii
John XXIII, and church of the poor, 40, 88
justice, for all, 104
justice of God, search for, 116-21

Keynes, John Maynard, on ethics and the economy, 98, 99
kingdom of God,
    and liberation theology, 72, 74
    proclamation of, 114-32
knowledge, fragmentation of, 110, 111

language, theological, 3, 4
Las Casas, Bartolomé de, 16, 40, 45
Latin America
    poverty in, 4-7
    proclamation of reign of God in, 7-10
Levinas, Emmanuel, and alterity, 91
liberation
    and freedom, 115-21
    levels of (social, political, from sin), 5

as manifestation of covenant, 71
and salvation, 17
liberation theology
    basic concepts of, 13, 14
    and capitalism, 68, 69
    and classical theology, 65-76, 78-82
    contrast with existentialist theologies, 14
    critique of, 76-82
    debate over, 6
    definition of, 17
    and democracy, 25
    European and Latin American perspectives, 22-31
    and European theologians, 56, 76
    and faith, 87
    future of, 32, 33
    as idol, 119
    in Latin American context, 6, 7
    and life of the church, 87, 88
    and Marxism, 22-25, 77, 78, 82
    method of, 19, 20
    misunderstandings about, 26
    necessity for, 54-57
    and the other, 121
    original approach of, 57-65
    origins, 54, 55
    and preferential option, ix
    as pure theology, 58, 59
    as reflection in service of God's liberating praxis, 13-22
    and social sciences, 19
    and socialism, 68, 69, 77, 78
    and spirituality, 50-53, 120, 121
    and structural sin, ix
    significance of, ix, x, 11
    sources of, 14, 15, 26, 27
    starting point of, 58, 64
    view of the human person, 66

Libertatis conscientia (CDF), 20
Libertatis nuntius (CDF), 19
lordship of God, and liberation
      theology, 20
love
   and faith, 62
   and praxis, 62
   universal, 6
Lubac, Henri de, 27
Lumen gentium
   and catholicity of the church,
      137, 138
   as source of liberation theology,
      14, 56
Lyotard, J. F., on great narratives of
      modernity, 108, 109

Marxism
   critique of religion, 60
   and liberation theology, 22-25,
      65, 66, 69, 77, 78, 82
metanarratives (great narratives), of
      modernity, 108, 110-12
modern and postmodern world,
      34-36, 106-13. *See also*
      postmodernity

natural resources, depredation of, 96
neoliberal economic theory, 25, 48,
      49, 67, 68, 94, 107, 118
nouvelle théologie, and liberation
      theology, 79, 80, 81

orthopraxis, and orthodoxy, 19
the other, and liberation theology,
      121-25

Peukert, Helmut, on hermeneutic of
      difference, 112
Pius XII, and social justice, 4, 5

pluralism
   religious, 37-38, 40
   theological, 4
Poma, Guaman, 40, 45
poor
   complexity of world of, 43-47
   critical theological reflection by,
      xi
   as dialogue partners of theology,
      26, 27
   economic and social exclusion of,
      101-6
   identity of and dialogue with,
      121-25
   idolization/idealization of, 119
   and immigration, 101
   invisibility of, 39, 44
   irruption of, 39
   participation in process of sal-
      vation, 73, 75
   as personal subjects in Gutiérrez,
      viii
   and rich, x; disparity between,
      102, 103, 105
   See also poverty
Populorum progressio (Paul VI), 14,
      99
postmodernity, 35, 36, 106-13
   and dissolution of metaphysics,
      109
   and fragmentation of knowledge,
      110-13
   and pluralism, 109, 110
poverty
   as challenge to faith, 38-43
   as challenge to theology, 102-4
   as death, 129, 130
   and globalization, 47-50
   and gospel, 18
   and hunger, 18

in Latin America, x, 4-7, 38-43,
65, 88, 104-6
material, spiritual, and as commitment to the poor, 88, 89
prayer, in Christian life, 10
preferential option for the poor, 27,
28, 88, 89
as axis of Christian life, 41-43
and God's gratuitousness, 89-92
in Latin America, 7-10
and liberation theology, ix
and spirituality, 51, 52
and universal magisterium of
church, 7

Rahner, Karl, 27
theology of grace of, and
liberation theology, 79, 80, 81
Ratzinger, Joseph, dialogue with
Gutiérrez, xiii
Razeto, L., on solidary economy,
127
Reagan, President Ronald, and
liberation theology, 23
reflection
critical, theology as, 64-76
hermeneutical, and liberation
theology, 70-73
pastoral-practical, and liberation
theology, 74-76
socio-analytic, and liberation
theology, 65-70
systematic-theological, and
liberation theology, 70-73
theological, 85, 86
reign of God
proclamation of, in Latin
American context, 7-10
search for, 116-21
See also kingdom of God

religion, and postmodern world,
112, 113
renewal movements, preceding
Vatican II, 11, 12
Rerum novarum (Leo XIII), 14
revelation
and liberation theology, 27
and Vatican II, 12
Ricoeur, Paul, on poverty, 47
Romero, Oscar, and Latin American
spirituality, 52

salvation
eternal, and earthly well-being,
79, 80
and liberation theology, 71-74
salvation history, and profane
history, 80
sin
levels of, and liberation, 17
social and personal, 17
structures of, in economy, 100,
101
social sciences
and liberation theology, 19
and socioeconomic reality, 5
socialism, and liberation theology,
68, 69, 77, 78
solidarity, ethic of, 125-29
spirituality
as following Jesus, 51, 120
and liberation theology, 50-53,
120, 121
synods, of Latin American bishops,
and liberation theology, 15,
56

Tertio millennio adveniente (John
Paul II), 89, 114, 126, 129,
130

theocentric option, and preferential
    option, 90, 91
theologian, role of, 2, 3, 10, 16
theology
    classical, methodology of, 61
    content of, 2
    contextual, 32, 54, 55, 86
    of creation and life, 130, 131
    as critical reflection, 64-76
    and evangelization, 2-4, 7
    and faith, 2
    inadequacy of formulations, 85
    and listening to divergent
        opinions, 7
    and proclamation of gospel, 84-
        92
    regional, and universal church,
        55, 56; *see also* theology,
        contextual
    role in ecclesial community, 1-10
    as service to church, 7
    theoretical and practical, 61, 62
    universal, 55
A Theology of Liberation (Gutiérrez),
        in history of theology, viii, ix,
        13, 57

theology of liberation. *See* liberation
        theology
theory, and praxis, 61, 62, 63, 64
Thomas Aquinas
    definition of theology of, 58
    on human yearning for God, 79,
        80
Toffler, Alvin and Heidi, 96

utopia, and economic order, 127,
        128

Vatican II, on human person, 12, 13
Vattimo, G., on modernity and
        postmodernity, 109
verticalism, 28
Vitoria, Francisco de, 16, 97

"we," as collective subject, in Europe
        and Latin America, 28-31
weak thought, 109, 110, 124
wealthy, and liberation theology, 20
Weber, Max, analysis of modernity,
        108, 109
women, and poverty, 44, 46